ISBN: 1-55306-117-9

...*ishing* is a Christian Book Publisher dedicated to further-
...of Christ through the written word. For more information,
...oira Street West, Belleville, Ontario, Canada K8P 1S3.
...hone: 1-800-238-6376. Fax: (613) 962-3055.
E-mail: info@essencegroup.com
Internet: www.essencegroup.com

Printed in Canada
by

Essence
PUBLISHING

A Man Worth Knowing

Rev. R.A. Bombay

A Mar
K

Cal R.

All Scripture
King James
Thomas Nels

Essence Publ
ing the work
contact: 44 M
P

Belleville, O

Table of Contents

Acknowledgments

This book would not have been possible without the help of many who knew Dick Bombay. I would like to acknowledge more than I can list, since many people have spoken to me of my father, and his influence on their lives.

Rev. Tom Johnstone, General Superintendent of the Pentecostal Assemblies of Canada, who worked closely with Dad. Rev. H.H. Barber, pastor of Calvary Temple in Winnipeg, who also worked with him in the governance of the P.A.O.C. at the national level. Rev. Gordon Upton, who was his Assistant Superintendent in the largest district of the P.A.O.C., Eastern Ontario and Quebec, and who also followed Dad into office as District Superintendent. David Mainse, President of the Crossroads Christian Communications, who knew Dad for what he was: a wise man of God.

My family, particularly my mother, Olive Bombay, who knew

Dad most intimately, speaks only good of him, denying that there ever was a bad side to him. Had someone else written this book, perhaps they could have found someone to speak about negative characteristics. I could find no one who would, or perhaps even could.

My siblings: David, Ruth, Lois, and Rick, together with our cousin Ken Bombay, offered invaluable insights from their own perspectives, and from their better memories.

And last, but certainly not least: God. I must acknowledge that I have never met a man over whom God had greater reign.

I never spoke to my father as Dick, but only as Dad. In this account, depending on the circumstances of the narrative, I refer to him variously as Dick, Dad, Pastor Bombay, etc.

I am privileged to have been a son of such a man as Dick Bombay.

Cal. R. Bombay

Introduction

From the poverty of a dirt farm in Northern Ontario where he
went barefoot to school until after the first few snowfalls, to
becoming the Assistant General Superintendent of the fastest growing Protestant denomination in Canada: a story that must be told.

Richard Gerald Austen Bombay! With a name like that, questions were sure to be asked. And it does make an interesting story,
including laughter, unspeakable hardship, and a few unsavoury
chunks of family history. But there was sheer grit and enough self-
confidence to make a difference. He came from a strong and united, but very dysfunctional family.

But primarily, there was God. God, who changed the direction
of a family.

This story is about only one son of that family: "Dick."

Genuine humility and a self-effacing nature characterized his life and ministry. Never one to promote himself, he respected authority, but when he had it, never abused it. A genuine love of people seemed to be the driving force behind his ministry. He learned to love as God loves – unconditionally.

This is not so much the story of one person, but perhaps more, the stories of the many people who came into contact with R.A. Bombay. He was a "Man Worth Knowing." He wrote:

"I am fearful of over-dramatization lest the simple truth be lost. What God does needs no exaggeration.... If writing this furthers the work of God in other lives, or in His Church, I shall be forever grateful to God, and to those who encouraged me to write.

"I have never made any claim to be a 'healer' or a 'worker of miracles' but these things do appear frequently, and just as they happened. Every Pentecostal minister has had, or should have, similar experiences. And why not? God still confirms His Word with signs following."

My attempt was to gather further information about my father, Dick Bombay, and to weave it into a clear story of his life and ministry. I pray this will encourage and help many.

1

The Mighty Hunter

The tension was high. There were between eight and ten of them. They were all barefoot and dressed in whatever was available. Mostly overly worn breaches, and shirts with rips and holes. They clutched their bows and arrows tightly, looking for movement behind any rock, any tree. Some of them had only sling shots and a handful of stones. There also was rope for climbing the ridges.

The enemy was just beyond the rock ridge ahead. They were sure of it.

Each of them had a little food, already squashed between slices of bread, hidden inside their clothes. They were already very hungry, but the tension of the moment took their minds off food completely. Suddenly, one of them let fly with a stone from his sling shot. The stone flew over the ridge. They watched closely, hoping to see a feathered head look over the ridge, hoping for a clean shot.

The one who sent the stone waited, tense… then, as the tension subsided, Dick shouted loudly to all the others, "Let's eat!" There was general agreement, and though it was only about mid-morning, they pulled out their whole day's supply of food and chewed it down, sitting in a circle, laughing and talking. For those few moments, the thought of the enemy was totally dismissed from their minds. Their slings shots, bows, and arrows set carelessly aside. After all, it was easier to carry their food in their stomachs than to continue crushing it under their bodies as they wiggled through the bush on their bellies toward their enemies.

They told stories of their accomplishments in battle. They lay down in the cool woods and traded lies. They were not meant to be lies, they were just imaginations running wild. Where was there ever a hunter, or a fisherman who didn't indulge in such fantasies?

They would get back to the enemy soon enough. They had all day. School was out for the summer, and only when they heard the whistle from Tenant's Saw Mill closing the day, did they realize it was supper time. They would reluctantly gather up their weapons and, on weary legs, go to their various homes, scarcely able to put one foot in front of the other.

When The Rev. Richard Gerald Austen Bombay, still only seven years old, got home, supper was over. His mother had left some food for him in the warming closet where he could help himself. It didn't take long for Dick to read himself to sleep (a habit he kept through his whole life).

By the time he awakened in the morning, the whole family, except his mother, had gone to their various chores. Dick, the youngest in the home, got up for some breakfast, and when the Tenant's Saw Mill whistle sounded, it was his signal to head out for another day, of tracking down that illusive enemy which they never did see. As many of the eight to ten boys as could turned up for this new day of adventure. A summer of great adventure in the north woods of Ontario. Muskoka – God's country!

Some strange and wonderful things happened on that old sandy farm. Dad would often fill our ears with the joys and sorrows, fears and fantasies, which filled his first nine years of life.

But every boy has a background, a history, a family which forms his thinking, his character, and his world view. My dad, Dick, had his share of background... probably more than his share!

Who would dream that this scruffy, poor, skinny kid, living out in the bush in a log cabin, the youngest of too many mouths to feed, would one day be called The Rev. Richard A. Bombay. Dick, to his friends. He didn't have any enemies... well... one maybe, but that changed too!

It was 1917 when this skinny kid practised his woods craft.

Some Strange Background

The story really starts in England, in Leeds, Yorkshire, when a man named John George Bumby (sometimes spelt Bunby, or Bumbee, which means "a quagmire" – not a promising beginning) decided, for reasons of his own and a great deal of pressure from his father, who was probably a vicar in the Church of England, to leave England. Whatever his father's occupation, he was a dedicated abolitionist. It seems John George came home drunk one night with the strong smell of liquor on his breath, and his father, being somewhat more than Victorian in his morality, decided that having once begun with strong drink, young John George was destined for a life of depravity and shame.

Rather than share such a vast potential for embarrassment with the whole family and the parish, it was decided to disinherit him, put a few hundred pounds at his disposal, and cashier him off to the colonies, as a "remittance man." Canada was the fortunate receptacle for such a thoroughly debased specimen of the human race. After all, his father was a temperance leader, and possibly The Vicar!

John George Bumby landed in North America with a steamer trunk and a hang-dog look. He probably went to several places, including Lockport, New York. But Canada was a land of promise, and after all, he was "rich," he had a few pounds sterling coming on a regular basis. He moved to Canada and took a wife who was part native. They took up residence on Scugog Island with Port Perry within sight across the waters of Lake Scugog.

We know very little about him. He was a well-known figure in the Port Perry and Scugog areas of Ontario. In 1871, he was buried on Scugog Island, but we're not sure where. Before he died, he sired a son born on August 16 of 1859 and called him William John Bumby (spelt Bombey in Scugog records). There were also two sisters, one called Jane, born "Febury" 6, 1857, and another called Matilldy, born May 15, 1862. Matilldy was remembered as Aunt Mime by the few who remembered any references to her.

So Dick had a grandfather he never knew! We know very little about old John George Bumby. We know that to get land on Scugog Island, he pulled a great scam. He picked the piece of land, harvested and sold the wonderful pine trees on it, then bought the land with the money from the trees he stole. Maybe a bit crooked, but no one ever accused him of being stupid. One can't really say he was religious either. He did own a little Bible with a few family records scratched in pen or pencil.

His marriage was a mess. Dysfunctional to such a degree that it was about to fall apart. Some say the only thing that saved their marriage was that John George died in a cholera epidemic. Even before that, some family history seems to indicate that the three children were "farmed out" at times. John George had a very serious drinking problem. What started in England carried through his life, marriage, and to his death. He was a drunkard.

But Old George did have that small Bible, which was stolen along with everything in the house when some crooks visited while Old George and his family were away for the day. Everyone suspected "The Crandles," a notorious family who ran a guest house – some of whose guests "disappeared." They rowed a boat from the Island to Port Perry on the shores of Lake Scugog "to get provisions."

By some weird twist of fate, Dick's older brother, Ed, fell in love with the thieves' granddaughter, Irene Crandle, who recognized the Bumby family name from an old unused Bible in the attic. She brought it down, showed it to Ed, who recognized all the family names and laid claim to both the Bible and the granddaughter. I have that Bible today.

The world into which Dick Bombay was born on September 4, 1910, was not the world we live in today. Like many families, there were secrets and some severe dysfunctional attitudes and habits.

Like any lad of his age, Dick knew what the word "bastard" meant. Its use was definitive and demeaning, and great shame was attached to being born out of wedlock. Richard (Dick) Gerald Austen Bombay was born a bastard, although he never knew it until he was 12 years old. William John's first wife, Susan, who was possibly a common-law wife, died on October 28, 1919, when Dick was nine. His father officially married Nettie two years after the funeral. The wedding was performed by Rev. John A. Keller in Saint Matthew's Parsonage on October 31, 1921. The witnesses were Harry and Annie Spencer. Thus, Dick and his five siblings became legitimate.

When the revelation of his illegitimate birth became known to Dick, it became a major and ever-present thought in the back of his mind. This shame plagued his mind for many years to come. It affected some major decisions in his life.

And the name "Bombay" raised some questions from time to time. It goes back to his father becoming an orphan.

The spelling of William John Bumby got twisted at the time of his father George's death on Scugog Island. In those days, when the husband died, the children were considered orphans. Later, in 1931, he was registered as William John Bumby by the Ontario Local Pension Authority. He worked as a servant to the Netherton family for three years until the age of eleven, then he was articled into the service of Dr. Harrison Haight as his driver and general "factotum." William John, known by his second name John, was twelve years old at that time, in April 1871.

Meanwhile, his mother, with his older sister, Matilldy, born in May of 1858, moved back to the States, married again, and was buried in Cleveland, Ohio. No trace has ever been found of his younger sister, Jane, born in 1859.

The name Bombay, according to Scugog township records, was Bombey in some of the records. John Bombay was orphaned along with his sisters, Jane and Matilldy, when John was about nine or ten. His father died in a cholera epidemic which swept through northern Ontario in early 1868. When Dr. Harrison Haight took John in as his "factotum" a few years after his father died, John, uneducated, did not know how to spell his name, and Dr. Haight wrote it down as Bombay. This registration took place at the time of William John's baptism on December 29, 1868. A simple mistake. Now we're all stuck with it.

Dick's father, John, was an inventive man, a jack-of-all-trades, able to fix anything it seemed. He was a careful worker and gained a government certificate as a qualified and registered engineer. He moved to Lockport, New York, where he lived with Susan Egglestone. Three children were born to them. Dick was not one of them. They were William, Bertha, and Sydney.

So where did Dick come from?

For reasons no one knows exactly, John and Susan separated, and John ran off with Susan's sister, Nettie. There seemed to be some tensions between John and his mother-in-law. Thus, they moved to Buffalo, New York, and eventually to the village of Thorold, near St. Catherines, Ontario. The children were all born and registered as Canadians. John fathered six more children with Nettie. They were Jessie Irene, John Edward (known as Ed), Lillian Amelia, George Albert, Dorothy May, and the last and final edition, Richard Gerald Austen – DICK. Dick was born in the village of Thorold, now a part of St. Catherines. In his own opinion, he was last and least.

In 1911, when Dick was nine months old, the whole family moved to Muskoka. This was mainly to escape the stigma attached to the adulterous relationship. They moved to a sand and rock farm in the bush about three miles outside of Bracebridge.

There were nine children in all, some of them well into their teens. There was a rock ridge right down the middle of the farm. They lived in a small, two-storey log house. No electricity and a wood stove for both cooking and heating. The only farming they did was garden vegetables for their own use, and enough to feed two pigs for the summers, their cow, and the horse they used for pulling the buggy in summer and the cutter in winter. The winters were harsh and the bedrooms cold.

One winter, the whole family survived on turnips with very little meat, if you can call a little bit of pork fat "meat." Sometimes the turnips were mixed with the wild berries gathered and preserved for winter.

To understand the man, you must understand the boy. His was not an unusual life for boys born shortly after the turn of the century. The economy and the work force was shifting more and more to industrial, and Dick's father, like most men of his day, was anxious to find work anywhere in order to support his large family. He was an engineer, and opportunities opened up in the more distant north country of Ontario, as well as back in St. Catherines. Meanwhile, the family eked out a bare existence on that old dirt farm.

Nettie was a "town woman" and never adapted well to living on the farm. It was too far from the town which had just a few more conveniences. Yet she worked hard at looking after the family, canning and cooking whatever they could grow or pick wild in the bush. Nettie, in spite of her past, or perhaps because of it, became a very devout woman in many ways. She read her Bible regularly. She became a strict prohibitionist, which once caused her great embarrassment.

She had canned a batch of wild berries for the winter months, and they had turned alcoholic. She threw them out on the garbage heap at the back of the house, where the chickens proceeded to peck away at them, becoming drunk, wobbling and falling all over. When Nettie came out to discover why her children were whooping it up and laughing so much, she tried to swear them to secrecy. After all, she was a "prohibitionist," and if this were to get out, she'd be the laughing stock of the district! The secret got out.

Dick's father, John, was often away for weeks and even months building bridges and doing others engineering jobs in the summer, and working in logging camps in the winter. The money he was able to send home was barely enough.

Some of the older children had moved into the town of Bracebridge, two of whom were working at Bird's Woolen Mill.

Every Family Has a Skeleton

Dick's father had been working as an engineer at the Welsh Grape Juice plant in St. Catherines for a long time, while the family lived on the farm. It was while the family was there that word came to John in St. Catherines that Dick's mother's sister, Susan, had died in New York state, and would be buried in Lockport, New

York. John, Dick's father, sent for his common-law wife, Nettie, to attend Susan's funeral with him. Dick had never ever met "Aunt" Susan, so her death meant little to him.

But, while his father and mother were attending the funeral in Lockport, George, Dick's older brother, told him the following account. These are the details he remembers:

Years before, his father, John, had worked in the United States and had become acquainted with the Egglestone family in Lockport, New York. There were several daughters, and after a long acquaintance with the whole family, John eventually married Susan Egglestone. Three children were born from this union: William, Bertha, and Sydney.

Apparently there was some kind of family problem, which Dick heard his father say was caused by Susan's mother. He did not know the details, other than that through the turmoil that ensued, John and Susan parted ways. At that time, a common-law relationship began with Susan's younger sister, Natalie (Nettie), which continued until Susan died in 1921. There were six children born during the common-law arrangement, Dick being the youngest.

Dick had no idea at all about this, though he was quite aware of the constant arguing, threats, and bitterness. He heard his father say to his mother such things as, "You know I don't have to stay with you!" Dick had no idea what caused all the acrimony.

When George, Dick's next oldest brother, told Dick that his parents were not married, and that all six of his siblings were born out of wedlock, he was shocked beyond description and felt great humiliation and mortification. It seemed his whole world had collapsed. George told Dick that this was well known, and that he was surprised Dick hadn't heard about it. Everyone else seemed to know!

For a long time, Dick thought he and all his siblings were looked down upon. In those days, illegitimacy was something of which to be greatly ashamed. And Dick was very ashamed, although he didn't remember ever having held any bad feelings toward his parents.

He remembers distinctly when the load of this shame lifted some years later. Rev. Bert Gunter, a Free Methodist minister, was invited to speak in a mid-week service in the little Pentecostal Church in Huntsville, where Dick worked at the time. Possibly he knew about the family background; but Dick didn't know for sure. He felt Rev. Gunter was speaking directly to him that night. "No matter who you are, who your parents are, no matter where you come from... when you come to Jesus, you are a new creation; old things have passed away. ALL things have become new!"

Dick had heard this before, of course, but that night the Spirit of God applied it to *him,* and his shame and humiliation passed totally from him. He has not trumpeted this story, yet it did affect some of the decisions he made throughout the years.

Notably, many years later, when he was nominated for election to become the General Superintendent of the Pentecostal Assemblies of Canada, to which office there was a good probability that he would be elected, he withdrew his name. He did not want the possibility to even exist that he could be an embarrassment to his Fellowship, should the press learn of his background. It was a contributing factor, although not the only one, to his withdrawing his name. We suspect he didn't feel worthy of the position.

He shared this with several of his very close ministerial friends, and with his family. It has been committed to paper for the first time, but only in the hope that it may help others who have laboured under a similar kind of shadow. Anyone may rise above the load as he has, and go on to serve the Lord, humbly and successfully.

Dick was a normal boy, at least that's what he told us, his children. Although he was the youngest in the home, he didn't fare too badly. Hand-me-down clothes were part of his lot, and it wasn't thought unusual in those days. All families did it. A new piece of clothing for the youngest in a family was as rare as a fresh orange. And that happened only at Christmas – sometimes.

He wasn't a bad boy, although he did have a terrible temper up until an experience that changed all that. About the worst thing he can remember ever doing was back on the farm. After moving into the town of Bracebridge, Dick returned to the farm for a visit with his close friend Clarence McEwen. It was only a three-mile walk.

Together, they wandered out behind the old stable, where they found the old buggy. It was in poor condition, but usable. It had been sitting there for a few years. Dick and Clarence were overcome with evil. They tore that old buggy apart, twisted the frame all 'round, knocked the spokes out of the wheels, and created general mayhem back on the old homestead.

He was never found out. His best sleep ever probably took place on October 20, 1988, when he finally confessed this horrible sin to me, his fifty-year-old son. The family never did find out what had happened, and concluded the buggy had been struck by lightning. And in that country, that was a real possibility. Lightning storms in Muskoka are spectacular!

Lightning struck a tree just seventy feet in front of Dick's face one day as he was watching a storm through the window. He saw it shudder, and, rather than simply fall over, it seemed to just crumble to the ground. Within a year it had rotted away to powder. Trunk, roots, and all were gone. Pine stumps usually get in the way for years.

That old farm, and the family, fun, work, and often fear of bears and wolves all contributed to his understanding of life, and to his intimate knowledge of the north bush. High Falls was not far away, and the fishing was excellent – in those days.

Neighbouring farms with their families with similar foibles made for a fascinating, if hard, up-bringing of a pre-teen like Dick.

There was a cemetery at the corner of the farm. In daylight, Dick was as brave as any gladiator of Rome, but at night, chills of terror would grip his young soul. There was a birch tree planted at the headstone of one grave, and the whisper of the wind through its leaves would crack his imagination wide open. It sounded to him like people trying to scratch their way out of the caskets beneath the sunken sod.

That same grave yard caused quite a commotion in the Bombay homestead one night. Ed, Dick's older brother, was courting Birdie Cooper just down the road at another farm, and on his way home had to pass the cemetery. There was a large boulder, with a flat top, just outside the gate. As he passed this rock, he saw his sister Bertha sitting on top of the boulder.

It scared him so badly, he ran at full speed the rest of the way home, burst through the front door of the house, and didn't stop until he'd slammed up against the back wall of the kitchen. He stood there white and shaking as he told the others what had happened. No one really knew what to think, because Bertha had been dead for seven years! Ed spoke of this incident right up until the time of his own death many years later. He never did marry Birdie Cooper.

It was two miles through the trees to the old school house, and Dick started in grade one. He spent four years in the same single-room school. When September came, school began. But the chores didn't end. He ran on bare feet all summer and, after the chores, ran barefoot to school. It wasn't until the snow fell that finally socks and shoes were added to his wardrobe.

3

The Big Move

When John was away at various jobs, Dick and his siblings were a tough assignment for a mother in such a rough environment, especially for a woman who stood no more than five feet three inches tall. The family was in the process of buying the farm.

A brother and sister were boarding in town where they worked, and attended both the Salvation Army in the mornings and the Methodist church in the evenings. The whole family came in for the Sunday meetings, buggy in summer, cutter in winter. If John was in a snit, he'd refuse to harness the horse, and the whole family would walk the three miles to church in town.

John would have nothing to do with church. But Nettie would lead in family devotions with Bible readings and prayer every evening. John would sit in the corner of the room smoking his pipe, grumbling and deliberately rattling the newspaper to try to annoy Nettie.

Town was attractive to Nettie.

As a city woman, she abhorred living in the country. No lighting except kerosene lamps. No new invention like the telephone. No protection from wild animals and the "hobos" who frequently tramped through the country roads. She was afraid of horses and cows, and avoided them when possible, leaving their care to the older children. She decided to move.

Without his father's knowledge or collaboration, Dick's mother moved to town into a rented house. One more winter out there without John to help when problems arose would likely kill them all. The rent in town was $4.00 a month for a little frame house just above the Muskoka River. Another family had moved out and it became available in 1919.

When John came home from his work in engineering somewhere or other, with a few dollars in his pocket, Nettie was there in town to meet him.

Dick's mother broke the news of the move to town in a rather remarkable way. To get back to the farm from the train, they had to pass down Woodward Street where they now lived in the newly rented house. John was limping along, stopping frequently because of weakness and pain – rheumatism. As they came in sight of their new "home," John saw that the once unoccupied house was now inhabited, and asked, "Who lives in Will's house?" Nettie, rather fearfully, answered, "The Bombays."

Without a word, "Pa" continued to trudge toward the house where he was able to drop into a chair in his "new" home. Everyone stood about nervously, expecting John to explode with temper and reproach for Nettie moving without his knowledge or consent. The subject had often come up in the past, and the firm answer was always, "NO." But now, not a word, and the family settled in to as peaceable a home life as they'd ever had. With a brother and sister and Dick's father working, the Bombays began to have a little more food on the table, and a few extras, like an orange each at Christmas time.

It wasn't long after this that one of the first miracles in the Bombay home took place. John was healed of his rheumatism and even more severe inner turmoil and problems. He had turned to the Lord for forgiveness and cleansing. "All things work together for good...."

John died in that same home, fifteen years later in 1934.

Dick remembered that move. He had to leave his school companions (fellow hunters) and go into town where he knew no one his own age. His elder brother William and a sister had been living in town, busy at Bird's Woolen Mills. He remembered the decision to buy the house, and the $4.00 monthly payments which were applied to the price.

Suddenly, this was all about to be lost. It doesn't seem like much now, but back in the "dirty thirties," it was a whole lot of money that they had already paid on the house and were about to lose.

The owner of the house had not kept the tax payments up-to-date. The house went up for sale. Somehow, through the Manager of the Bank, prior word was received by the family, and they were able to scrape enough money together to buy the house and avoid eviction.

It was all paid off before Dick's mother died.

The neighbours, new to the Bombays, had warned Mrs. Bombay that everyone in the neighbourhood knew the house into which they had moved was haunted. The whole family was made aware of the "hants what were in that house." As a matter of fact, there were noises and strange sounds which could not be explained, but the Bombays had no fear. Well, most of them....

One hot, moonlit summer night, Dick and George, who shared a room, were jolted into wakefulness by the yowling of a cat in the great pine tree just outside their window. After throwing almost everything that wasn't nailed down at the cat, the yowling and screeching continued. George and Dick headed for the woodpile downstairs to get larger pieces of ammunition to throw at the cat.

At the bottom of the stairway was a window facing the tree. Bright moonlight flooded the outdoors. George, the older, was ahead of Dick, and as soon as he got to the bottom of the stairs, he let out a shriek, streaked up the stairs past Dick, yelling, "Pa... Pa... Pa... PAAAAA." Dick was frozen for a moment, then went to see what had caused George's rapid retreat.

Three figures robed in white stood under the tree, rhythmically lifting and dropping their arms, poking at the cats with fishing poles. They may have looked like ghosts, but in fact were Dick's two older sisters and another girl who boarded at the house. The cats had ruined their sleep, too.

By this time, Dick's dad was shambling down the stairs, hauling on his pants and demanding to know what all the commotion was about. Dick was laughing fit to kill, which only added to the confusion. Finally, the story all came out and "Pa" rescued George from under the covers where he was still muttering, "ghosts, ghosts, ghosts."

Ma had lit a lamp, and the whole household sorted out the action. George never really did appreciate the humour of that night!

Town life was a little different. Doctors and medicine were not plentiful, even in town, but John, having been raised by Dr. Haight for some years, and living close to the Indian people of Scugog Island as a child, had learned a few cures of his own. When anyone in the family got the flu, or a common cold, or even pneumonia, out would come the "galongall" made from some root. It was a terribly bitter thing, especially when you had to take a whole spoonful when you were already sick. But it seemed to work. Dick later found out it was sold in drugstores under the name "Wrangle Root." It was awful stuff, but you can't argue with success!

They didn't have cures for quite a few things, one of which was "mange." When a cat got mange, you had to get rid of the cat. Dick was assigned the duty one time, and along with his new friend in town, Ernie Kennedy, Dick put the cat in a strong gunny sack, with a bunch of rocks, and sank it in the Muskoka River behind the house. They killed the cat before they put it in the river. Several days later, however, that same cat came crawling up the shore to the house yowling all the way, and it still had the mange. Obviously, that wasn't the cure. They had to kill it again. It was a bit like our sinful nature: hard to put to death.

Some strange things did happen in that little two-storey frame house. This is a story Dick, my dad, told me while we were sleeping in that old frame house, years later. We had gone up to cut big pine trees off the lot on the steep slope down to the Muskoka River behind the house.

Dick and his pa were sitting in the front room reading one night. The bedroom door wouldn't stay closed. They heard a "click." The latch on the bedroom door had suddenly jumped, and the door slowly swung open, hitting the foot of the bed inside. Dick's dad said, "Shut the door, Dick." Dick got up and shut the door. They read on for a few minutes.

"Click." The door opened again, and this time Dick made certain the latch had caught. A few minutes later, "click," and the door swung open again.

Dick's dad was an engineer. He knew how to use tools, and now he was annoyed. He got his tools, took the whole latch and face plate off, and refitted the whole assembly onto a new position on the door. He closed the door, put his tools away, sat down to read, and "click," the door swung open again. It kept clicking and swinging open the rest of the time they lived in that house. Perhaps the house did have "the hants"!

When my father told me that story, I kept my eye on that door all evening. I was about fourteen at the time.

But there were other odd things that happened, too. For instance, the stairs leading up to the bedrooms above were very creaky. Again, Dick, his dad, and his brother George were there sitting in the front room reading. They heard movement in the back kitchen and called out asking who was there. No one answered. No one else was in the house. Then they heard the steps creaking and footsteps go up the stairs. The stairs were in full view of the room, and there was no one there. Then the footsteps went across the floor upstairs, and they heard the springs of a bed squeak. George, terrified beyond fear, rushed up the stairs to see who was on the bed – no one anywhere!

As a result, it was no wonder when, a few weeks later, George came screaming down those same stairs. He said he saw a ghost outside his window trying to get in. As it turned out, it was the branch of a tree brushing the window in the breeze. But who can explain the other?

There was a great deal of fun mixed with work at that old frame house. Cutting ice from the Muskoka River down the hill at the back of the house was a fond memory. It would be hauled up to the ice house, covered with saw dust, and would serve all summer as the source of ice for the ice box in the house.

That same river was cleared of snow and used for hockey, and Dick recalled with great admiration the fact that the locally famous Toronto Maple Leaf player, "Ace" Bailey, got his start on that patch of the Muskoka River. Athletes were not considered to be even remotely godly in those days, but when Ace was almost fatally injured, the churches in town for the first time publicly prayed for him, an athlete. He recovered, but never played hockey again.

In summer, that same river provided an endless source of entertainment and fun for the family, especially for the younger children. The river didn't warm up until June or early July. When it did, they all took to the water. Dick, along with several others, had attended Boy Scouts, learning all about swimming safety, tying knots, canoe safety, and even "artificial respiration."

The river widened into a large bay just behind their house at the bottom of the long wooded bank. "Running logs" was one of the favourite pastimes for the local youngsters, even though very dangerous. Green pine logs are very slippery, and they collected in the bay from the logging up-river. Dick once slipped off the logs, went under the water, and the logs closed over his head. If Ernie Kennedy had not seen him go under, ran and parted the logs for Dick to get up for air – this story would never have been told.

When the mill had processed most of the logs, the bay became clear, and just above it was a narrow area where the river rushed through between the Bombay property and Flat Rock, on the other side. The ultimate test was to swim across the narrows. Ernie and Dick made it across, then George tried. George was never a strong swimmer, and the current got him, taking him into a wide part of the river they called "the bay." George panicked and started screaming for help. Dick and Ernie rescued him and were just pulling him up onto the bank when "Pa" came painfully stumbling down the bank in response to the terror in George's voice. It kind of spoiled the rest of their day.

They would make rafts of stray logs, tying them together with rope. Near drownings took place on a regular basis. The raft and stray logs often figured in the rescues, and parents rarely heard of the incidents. A small boy called Buzz persisted in taking chances, and after Dick rescued him twice, he warned him, "If you do it again, I won't pull you out." He never did it again.

Years later, Dick was met by a stranger who said, "You don't know me, do you?" Dick answered, "No, I'm afraid I don't." "You ought to," he said. "You pulled me out of the river twice when I was a kid." Dick had a little reunion with Buzz Brazier.

All the while, the family, never including "Pa" John, attended the Salvation Army meetings.

Because of the poverty, it was essential that Dick join the work force in the home. At a young age, he, with his father, took out a contract for wood-cutting, all by hand crosscut saw, for a neighbouring farmer. With axe and wedges, they cut 120 cords. They stayed in a tumble down shack during the week while they worked, with snow drifting in through the cracks onto them while they slept. Dick told of how he could see the stars through the roof of that shack. On weekends, they went back into town where it was warmer.

Their next job was in a stone quarry. Working in a stone quarry was not Dick's idea of a life-long job. But it was the only job available at that time. Dick was a general roustabout, shovelling coal and being the "powder monkey." That simply meant he loaded the drilled holes with blasting powder and set the caps for the explosion. The power had to be tamped with a wooden ramming pole. He had heard of explosions which blew off men's hands and killed some in the process. He was scared spitless. The boss saw that he was tamping too gently, and he took the pole from Dick and said, "You have to tamp it down hard," as he rammed the wooden pole onto the powder. Dick learned later that it would take stronger tamping than either could do to set it off. Setting the caps was the dangerous part.

Meanwhile, his father did the engineering part of the job, sharpening the rock drills and fixing everything and anything mechanical. He was very inventive. Once, the water jacket around a pump cylinder had frozen, cracking both the inner and outer jackets. It would take weeks to replace. John thought about it for a while, then sent Dick to the hardware store with a short list of materials, including a tap die and copper rods. Within half a day, he had the jackets so tightly sealed that work began again. It held the pressure right up to 110 pounds which was enough to operate the drills. A good thing too, since the place operated on a shoe string, and it would have put many a man out of work – and perhaps closed it forever.

They produced granite for tombstones and expensive building decorations. But the Depression killed the business, and the father and son team were without work again.

Within days, Dick found a job in Huntsville in the beam house of a tannery. A most foul-smelling and dirty place. He had to pull 80 to 100-pound cowhides about 2,200 times a day. He'd return to his boarding house exhausted after ten-hour days, six days a week. He worked there for two years, and was then transferred to a branch tannery in Bracebridge, which brought him home again.

He almost got killed by a faulty electrical switch which no one had taken the time to warn him about. It was to turn on a 500 HP motor which drove all the belts for the whole beam house. Dick threw the switch. He got the whole charge which threw him about twenty feet up against a pillar. Other employees came running and helped him to his feet. The boss came, asked him how he felt, then, without waiting for an answer, sent him straight back to work. Dad doesn't know how he ever made it through that day. There was no such thing as pay for any time off for any reason, and certainly no workman's compensation in those days.

By this time, some of the Bombays had "got religion, real bad," according to some.

Something happened which left a profound impression on Dick's mind. As a child of nine, Dick was saved in Sunday School in the Salvation Army. It was customary to periodically hold what they then called "Decision Sunday." The lesson for that particular day was Joshua's declaration:

"As for me and my house, we will serve the Lord."

Dick determined to make that same decision as best as he knew how. His Sunday School teacher prayed with him as he knelt, and he felt the peace of God come into his young soul. God's Spirit witnessed to him that he belonged to Him. It was very real to him, and he knew that he had became a child of God.

Not much attention was paid to children in those days. They were expected to "be good." Sometimes Dick was and sometimes he was not, but the Lord stayed by him. After his fifteenth birthday, he made an even more definite commitment of his whole life to God. This took place in a house prayer meeting. Dick spoke about that time: "I have not been perfect, but I have never backslidden since that day."

He drank of the water of life for the rest of his life. It's a well that never goes dry.

4

Religious Fanatics

Almost everyone belonged to some church in those days. There was a universal respect for God, though good preachers were few and far between. Sunday was definitely a day of rest, and woe betide anyone taking liberties! Stores were closed tight, and most windows were even covered to forestall window-shopping. Every church in town held their standards high.

There were many people in most of the churches who had a living faith in Jesus Christ and could point to a moment in their own lives when they had embraced Jesus as Lord and Saviour. On the other hand, some of the pulpits had lost conviction and power through the first inroads of higher criticism and modernism.

One of the strong evangelical congregations in Bracebridge was the Salvation Army. The Bombay children were firmly escorted to Sunday School and Morning Services every Sunday by Mother. It was in the Salvation Army that Dorothy, George, Ed, and Dick came into a personal relationship with Jesus Christ. A great love and loyalty grew in their hearts for their church, and Sunday was not the chore that it seemed to many others.

It was into this comfortable and happy monotony that a new breed of religion suddenly appeared. Dick was a typical twelve-year-old, on a typical Saturday night in Bracebridge that one particular evening. Shopping was the usual activity for most families, and socializing with other townsfolk was their entertainment. If the weather was good, Saturday evenings took a long time. The streets were crowded with people, horse-drawn carriages, and the occasional motorcar; dirt streets and no curbs, just board walks at the front of the stores. The main street was just gravel at best, and mud when it rained. It was 1922.

His mother, older sister Dorothy, and Dick heard the sound of music. It was unusual and caught their attention, along with that of many other folk from town and the country around who had come in for the evening of shopping and socializing.

About a dozen people stood in a circle right in front of the Bank of Nova Scotia (the bank is still there). Dick remembers an autoharp, a guitar, and a tambourine. The song was strange and new. He had never heard anything like it before!

"I do believe without a doubt,
The ark is comin' up the road.
God's people have a right to shout
For the ark is comin' up the road."

A lady dressed in a long white dress, who seemed to be the leader of the group, was shaking the tambourine and skipping and tripping up and down in the circle within the ring of people.

They probably sang other songs the Bombay family knew, but this one stuck in Dick's head.

They watched and listened. One after another, people in the group told what God had done for them. This was not unusual to the Bombays, since they attended a church where testimonies were common, but these testimonies were most uncommon! In addition to testimonies of salvation, these people were talking about how they had received the baptism of the Holy Ghost and spoke in tongues! Some of them even reported miraculous healings: an immediate knitting of a broken arm; an old woman raised up instantly from the last stages of pneumonia, in answer to prayer. There were several rather remarkable reports!

Dick's mother was a rather blunt little woman. After the meeting was over, she went straight up to the apparent leader and asked, "Can you heal my daughter?" The lady replied, "No, we can't heal anyone, BUT JESUS CAN!"

Mother explained that Dick's sister had some sort of repulsive running sores all over her body, and that it had lasted for several years. Doctors had tried various remedies but nothing had helped, and she had to be taken from school because of her condition and appearance.

The lady said they were having a tent meeting the next day, Sunday, and that they should bring Dorothy there for prayer.

So, they went!

At the end of the afternoon meeting, they took Dorothy forward for prayer. Others had also come forward for prayer. It was all somewhat strange and exciting. They actually saw some healings take place, but nothing appeared to happen to Dorothy. They went home wondering.

But they did see the miracle. By Thursday that week, all her sores had dried up. There were no scars left, and her skin remained clear for the rest of her life.

Shortly afterward, Dick's brother George was healed of an injury caused by the falling of an elevator gate. His father was instantly healed of stomach ulcers and ate his first hearty meal in months, yet he still never gave God any place in his life. He seemed to shy away from anything to do with the church – any church.

And then Dick's turn came.

He had never been a robust child. He had some sort of heart condition, and when he was about ten years old, he developed a thyroid condition. It was quite common in that area. It was said to be due to a deficiency in their drinking water. Shortly before, Dick had been a pallbearer for a neighbour boy who had died during surgery for his thyroid.

The thyroid condition affected Dick's heart even more, which severely limited his activities. He missed a lot of school because of it. As well, he had severe nosebleeds, and his nerves were affected to the point that he would have nightly delirium. The most prominent result of the thyroid condition was diagnosed as a goitre by the school nurse. It was quite visible. Grade eight in school was missed because of this sickness, and Dick dropped behind his schoolmates.

One Sunday afternoon, Dick's mom took him forward for prayer. Nothing seemed to happen, and he went to bed as usual that night.

The next morning at breakfast, Dick's dad suddenly burst out, "My God! Look at that boy's throat!" It wasn't an oath, but an outburst of pure amazement and joy.

Dick reached for his throat, and all evidence of the swollen goitre was completely gone. Everyone in the family felt Dick's neck, and the excitement was infectious. A real miracle had taken place, and Dick was able to swim and play ball that summer without nosebleeds. That winter he skated and played hockey with no ill effects. Every subsequent medical examination Dick had, right into old age, has verified his freedom from any thyroid problems. Dick pointed to this experience as having saved him from a life of sickness and probably early death. And, to quote him, "That is why I want to serve Him as long as I live." He served God in ministry well into his eighties.

In those same tent meetings, a neighbour, Mrs. Jeffries, came forward for prayer. Her story is similar to the woman spoken of in Luke 13:11,

> *...who had a spirit of infirmity eighteen years, and was bent over and could in no way raise herself up.*

She was anointed with oil, and the evangelist said to her, "Look up, sister!" The reaction was electrifying! For the first time in years she lifted up her head and, right before their eyes, her crooked back was made straight, and she stood tall. The kids had never guessed she was so tall. A great shout went up, and even the town drunk raised his hands, praising God with tears running down his face. They had seen the Kingdom of God come among them.

Those were exciting days. And the meetings went on.

Eventually, the weather became too cold to meet in the tent, so Dick's parents invited them to hold the meetings in their home. The Bombays continued to attend the Salvation Army in which most of the family were members. Some of the family were filled with the Holy Spirit, with the evidence of speaking in other tongues (read Acts 2). Others from the Salvation Army were also filled with the Spirit of God, as well as Christians from other churches.

New life came into the churches. The Salvation Army Captain invited the evangelist to hold a special week of meetings in the church, and many were saved, healed, and filled with the Spirit.

By this time, the church was full to overflowing in every service. This continued long after the evangelist, Mrs. Sharpe, had gone. The former Salvation Army Captain was happy to see the church thriving, filled, and blessed. His father had been a Methodist preacher and had told him about meetings like this.

But a new Captain came to pastor the Salvation Army hall. As with Israel in Egypt, "there arose a Pharaoh that knew not Joseph." He had no idea what "the Baptism in the Holy Spirit" was.

The new Captain did not favour what was happening. In spite of this, the revival continued, and more people were saved and blessed. They had to begin bringing in extra chairs to fill the aisles.

At the close of one service, it came as a great surprise when the altar had been filled with people seeking God, and the new minister literally shoved some of the people toward the door and announced, "There will be no more speaking in tongues in this place."

The only time anyone had spoken in tongues had been at the time they were first filled with the Spirit. No one had ever spoken aloud during a service, nor had anyone been boisterous or offensive in any way, although some raised their hands in praise as they sang their hymns.

When they had been pushed out to the street, the door was locked, and they were left bewildered. There were more than a dozen, although many others had also been filled with the Spirit.

All of them had been accustomed to attending church on an evening during the week, and three times on Sunday. Now they had no place to go; what were they to do? It was finally agreed that the rest of the folk should come to the Bombay home for a mid-week service. Others who had been "invited" to leave several of the other churches in town also came. That was the first separate meeting of Pentecostals in Bracebridge. Not by choice, but by force of circumstances.

They had no pastor, so they did all they knew to do – sing their old songs, pray, testify, read the Bible, and pray again. The Spirit of God moved on them in unusual ways. When it was time to go home, someone asked, "What will we do on Sunday?" Again it was agreed that they should meet in the Bombay home. "Pa" made himself scarce. Later they gathered in other homes. This practice continued for some time.

It seemed that God had set His own seal on that little growing group. God raised up a preacher from among them: Dick's older brother George. He was the oldest male member of the group who was saved. The growing group had many mature women, but it was decided George should be their "pastor." The first sermon he preached was from Psalm 73. He was expounding on every verse, at length. Finally someone pulled his coat-tail to bring him to a close.

From the time he was filled with the Spirit, he had a ministry of exhortation. God opened his understanding so that he could minister the Scriptures. He soon became the recognized leader, although he was one of the youngest of the group.

There was no intention of starting a church. Under God, it just happened! Their home was small, and when the crowd grew, others opened their homes, but it was soon recognized that any house was too small to hold all the people who were being saved and blessed and joining the group.

It was then decided to rent a vacant church in the centre of town. "Pastor" George continued to do most of the preaching, though it was not by his choice! He still had a full-time job. Sometimes other ministers were invited to come, but some of them did more harm than good. Dick became the unofficial assistant pastor to his brother George. George had no high school education. Dick was still attending, working, and assisting George. Most did not have much education. The forming of this "church" was for the simple reason that they had no organization which could recommend preachers to them. As a result, they looked for help from anyone who seemed interested in helping.

When the little church became too small to accommodate the constantly growing crowd, they rented an empty hall. They filled it with chairs, an old pump-organ, a pulpit, and a bench for an altar. George continued to be the "pastor." Although he had been working at the tannery since he was thirteen, George now devoted all his spare time to ministry. He had only a grade eight education, having given up school so that his younger sister Dorothy and the youngest, Dick, could go to high school. Dorothy chose not to go, but Dick did go to high school.

George began to get invitations to preach elsewhere, as his ministry became recognized and known. Dick helped him as much as he could when George was elsewhere preaching. He was also working full time at the tannery, but did what he could in the new "church."

One Sunday evening, George told the group he was leaving. He was planning on being gone for at least two years. He had been asked to go to Huntsville to take over a church Ma Sharpe had pioneered. He had also received invitations to conduct revival meetings in several other towns and cities. The whole group knew that these plans were being made but had not been able to answer the question, "Who will be our next pastor?"

Without even asking him if he would do it, George announced that Dick would be the pastor! Dick was only seventeen and had spoken in the meetings only a few times, mainly just reading the Bible. But, since the people were happy about it and Dick had some high school education, and since no one could think of an alternative, Dick did it.

He remained as pastor for more than two years, still working full time during most of that time. And the church continued to grow as God continued blessing them.

At the end of two years, Dick began to get invitations to hold revival meetings as well. Huntsville invited him for a week of meetings. His boss at the tannery, though not a Christian, was favourable. Dick's sister Dorothy went with him to help for the first weekend. There seemed a great hunger for God, and many people came to new life in Jesus Christ. One old man who had been saved from a life of sin, debauchery, and drunkenness came to say goodbye on the last Sunday evening. He said, "Brother Dick, I see they did not take up any offering for you." He took out a fifty-cent coin and said, "It's all I've got, but I want you to have it. You've done me good, God bless you."

In those days, that's how it was – and for many years to come. Dick counted the cost and determined to follow Jesus. Some years later, with a wife and two children, his records show that his income for some time averaged $1.37 a week. He did all the pastoral work, including looking after the church building. Even then, $1.37 wasn't much.

For a few years, he went from church to church, following the invitations which he received. These were all independent churches, many of them started in much the same way the congregation in Bracebridge had begun. He held no credentials but was simply known by the ministry God had given him. He never once had to ask for a place to preach.

It was difficult for him to believe, but Dick was "in the ministry."

5

Water? In the Dry Well?

Some rather remarkable things happened in the Bombay home which were part of the formation of the faith that both Dick and George would preach for the rest of their lives. Each incident, in its own way, was a formative influence in their ministries as they saw God at work in their own home and circumstances.

After living on the farm outside Bracebridge for nine years, and having moved into the house at the edge of town on Woodward Street, they had a problem. The only water supply they had was from a stone-cribbed well, about sixty feet from the house. The only alternative was the Muskoka River which was down a steep and long wooded hill. Every year, late in summer, the well went dry. This meant that Dick and the other kids had to carry water, for general purposes, up from the river in the valley behind the house. Dick's duty was to carry the drinking water from the nearest neighbour who was connected to the town water supply.

Visiting Pentecostal ministers always stayed at the Bombay home. They often recounted "the wonderful works of God," which included stories of how God brought water into several farm wells, in answer to prayer. This, of course, interested Dick because of the daily lugging of water when the well went dry.

One day, Dick asked a visiting evangelist, "Can you pray water into our well?" She later told him how startled she was to be asked such a question from a twelve-year-old boy, but her immediate and definite response was, "What God has done for others, He will do for you."

With their parents, they gathered around the windless housing and prayed. They didn't look into the well immediately after prayer, but on the weekend, Dick's mother went to Huntsville to visit. At that time, regular Pentecostal meetings had not yet begun in Bracebridge, so the family went elsewhere for meetings whenever possible.

Nettie had been reading a book entitled *An Irish Saint* about a woman known widely as "Holy Ann." This book gave an account of water which filled a well in answer to prayer. Nettie went to Huntsville, both to visit Dorothy and to attend the meetings where "Ma Sharpe" was preaching. After the meeting, Nettie and Ma Sharpe agreed in prayer for water in the Bombay well. Nettie went to stay overnight with her daughter.

While Dick's mother slept at his sister's home in Huntsville, she had a dream. In her dream, she saw herself drawing water from the well. As a result, she awakened and came home on a much earlier train than planned, arriving long before sunrise. She went straight to the kitchen and, without changing into a house dress, took out two water pails – making an awful racket at two o'clock in the morning. The family was aroused, wondering what was going on.

Pa, Dick's father, said to the whole family, "I told you your ma's gone crazy with that new religion!" Nettie paid no attention, went out to the well and hooked one of the pails onto the windless. She let it drop until she heard it splash into water. She drew up a full pail of clear, clean water. She let down the other pail, with the same result.

She hurried into the house, set the two pails of water on the stand, then told the whole of her dream and how she had set out to see if it was true. But there was the water! The well had been dry. It was late summer, and normally the well would have stayed dry until October.

The well never went dry again, ever! It was their water supply, and that of many neighbours whose wells continued to go dry every summer, until the town extended water pipes along Woodward Street, which at that time was the border of the town. All the neighbours knew this, and it became a conversation piece among them for years.

There is a picture of Nettie and Pa standing beside the well-housing, pointing up to heaven, "from whence cometh every good and perfect gift." Because it was a cool place, the well was later used as a refrigerator for milk, butter, and meat long after the town water supply had been hooked up to the house.

The well-housing finally decayed, and many years later when Dick had bought back the old homestead, although there was still water in the well, he filled it in to prevent accidents to children who might wander over the old boards on top.

Sweat and Growth

Dick had one particularly fond memory of that period in his life. He was one of the fortunate few who was able to get a job for the summer: building an addition onto the combined public and high schools. He was the "brick cooler," among other occasional duties. The bricks were being used so fast, they were being delivered from the brick factory right out of the ovens, and they were too hot to handle. Dick sprinkled and cooled them with water.

He was asked by the brick layers to do certain other little jobs, but when he was asked to go buy some beer for one bricklayer, he refused. He didn't think the boss would approve, nor did he want to be seen in a liquor store. The whole town knew he was a Christian, though just in his early teens at the time. After all, he was supposed to carry water for drinking, even if some of the workers did like a bit of oatmeal in it, but not beer.

One day, the same bricklayer who didn't get his beer called Dick to come up to the top of the wall at the front of the building. The bricklayer looked around guiltily, then invited Dick to help him lay the capstone. "I want you to have something to remember and to tell your children later," he said. With great pride, Dick mortared and levelled the capstone under the watchful eyes and helpful hands of his friend. For years, Dick drove by that high school, glancing up at that capstone and entertaining a secret grin. He told me the story and pointed to that capstone when I was about fifteen.

A year or so after this, because of financial pressures in the home, he left high school and went to work in Huntsville. He attended the meetings in the local assembly and taught a class of boys. They had no pastor, so Dick helped lead the young people's meetings. Sometimes he was asked to lead the song service. He played the guitar and the trumpet.

Being without a pastor, it was necessary for various adults to take turns in speaking. By common consent, one sister assumed leadership, and it was she who chose the various speakers. One day, because someone who had been asked to speak failed to appear, Dick was asked to read a Scripture and say a few words.

That day at work, Dick had been meditating on a certain passage of Scripture, and a few thoughts had parked in his mind. So he read that portion and rather lamely began to express the thoughts which had gone through his mind earlier in the day. He didn't get far! Suddenly, the Spirit of God came upon him, and without any effort on his part, words poured from his mouth.

He says of this experience later: "I didn't speak long, and when I just as suddenly finished, I was very embarrassed. I quickly left the platform to go and sit in the back seat. I just wanted to get out of sight. To my astonishment, I met the whole congregation going forward to pray around the altar. I sat in the back seat. I wanted to flee, but instead, I went back to the front and joined the others in prayer at the altar."

Some spoke to Dick afterward and assured him that the hand of God was on him for the ministry. He recalls: "It was then that I suddenly recalled that when I was first saved, in 1919, God had put a desire in my heart to be a preacher some day."

It had begun to come to pass. This experience had a profound impact on his life.

It was only a short time after this that he returned home to Bracebridge to work. And after a very short time, his brother George made the surprise announcement that Dick would be the pastor of his own home church.

Dick had begun preaching when he was barely sixteen years of age. When his older brother George, who was pastor of the local assembly, decided he was called into evangelistic work and was leaving the church, he announced that Dick Bombay was the new pastor. Dick was dumfounded! Shocked into total silence! George would not be there the next Sunday. He had neither consulted Dick on the matter, nor had anyone else, and he was taken completely by surprise. To say that he was plumb scared would be the understatement of the decade. He couldn't even describe his feelings.

However, the people accepted George's word, and Dick was thrust into the ministry. He continued to hold down his full-time job at the tannery, since there was no financial support from the church. It was all they could do to pay the rent for the hall and the utilities. He would save from his own wages until he had enough to afford an evangelist to come in and give them some "special meetings."

Once, when a couple of young preachers came, Dick bought each of them a new suit. The badly worn suits they came in were not conducive for respect of their message! But, that's just the way it was in those days. While he pastored that congregation from 1927 to 1930, he continued to hold down his full-time job, sixty hours a week.

6

Encouragement

A young fellow of seventeen years and a few months, without the benefit of Bible college, seminary, or even well-informed elders, needs encouragement from time to time. The occasional mention of a belief that God's hand was on Dick's life was hardly enough to totally convince him that "The Ministry" was where he belonged, in spite of his impressions when he was a nine-year-old.

And yet, here he was, "pastoring" a church! The fact that it was in his own home town only made it more difficult. And how many other pastors in town held down a full-time, back-breaking, sixty-hour per week job at the same time? It was bad enough that the other more established and elderly and theologically-trained pastors in town did not recognize him as a pastor at all. In fact, they rather frowned on him.

Dick was still living at home with his parents and his older sister Dorothy. He was just one of the neighbourhood boys, in a neighbourhood which knew everyone's business. It was one thing that the Bombay family should be all wrapped up in this "new religion," but that the seventeen-year-old son, the youngest of the family, would assume to be a pastor?

But not all the neighbourhood had discouraging attitudes. Across the block there lived an old couple. The husband, Joe, was a Christian. His wife, Mrs. Curran, was a shrew. She was often heard berating Joe as he went about his outside chores. It was not hard to imagine what he suffered within the confines of the house. But Joe seemed to bear all this patiently.

Added to his troubles, "he was old and feeble and grey, and bent with the chill of a winter's day." He limped with rheumatism and had lost one eye in an accident many years before.

Joe loved the house of God. He loved the fellowship of the saints. Regardless of the weather, he went to church during the week, and twice on Sunday. He walked slowly, but would start early so he could be there to welcome others and speak a cheerful word.

Dick does not recall ever hearing him complain, though he had much in his life and home to make him sad.

In those days, the pastor was expected to "close up" and see that everything was ready for the next meeting. Joe would often sit patiently until Dick was ready to leave, and then they would walk slowly home together. Joe's house was first, then Dick would continue on to his own.

At only seventeen years of age, Dick knew that he didn't have a great deal with which to "feed the flock of God," but as they walked home, Joe would pick out something Dick had said and make it sound, at least to Dick, as though he had expounded great pearls of wisdom and inspiration! Joe would often remark, "You done me good, you done me good." Few people in the north spoke English with proper grammar. But Joe spoke it with solid encouragement.

Oddly enough, this did not give Dick what he called "cranial hypertrophy," as happens to some preachers (which, interpreted, means "a swelled head"). On the contrary, it humbled him to think that this elderly saint, who had listened to some of the best preachers of his day, would listen with appreciation to Dick Bombay! Joe had little educational advantage and no formal Bible training, but his words of encouragement meant more to Dick, the young preacher, than he ever knew, though Dick always thanked him for his kind words.

Towards the end of his life, Dick often thought of Joe Curran. As he grew older, Dick made it a point to speak words of encouragement to God's servants, whether young or old. One wonders how many young men have failed in the ministry because there was no "Joe Curran" to give them a lift now and then.

That is one kind of encouragement. It came from a man.

But there is another kind of encouragement which comes from God, and every preacher looks for it! The Bible says that miracles should follow the ministry of God's Word. Dick wanted, and needed, to see this confirmation from God – if he was truly separated to the ministry!

An Answer to Prayer

In 1929, Dick had a remarkable answer to prayer which encouraged him in what he was pretty sure was his "call" to ministry. He was pastoring his home church in Bracebridge and, at the same time, still had the full-time job in the factory.

The wife and teenage daughter of his boss at the factory were members of his church. Though his boss did not profess to be a Christian, he was inclined to be favourable. When Dick asked for two weeks off work to hold evangelistic meetings in the Huntsville church, which was without a pastor at the time, he readily gave his permission. Dick's older sister Dorothy came on the weekends to help him in the meetings.

They had met for prayer on Saturday evening, and a little girl appeared at the meeting with a note from her mother. It was asking that they come and pray for the little girl's fourteen-year-old brother who was very seriously sick. They followed the little girl to her home, which was not very far from the church.

The boy lay on a bed. He was emaciated and had a very high fever; they could actually feel the heat rising from his wasted body. His fingers and arms were just skin and bones. His eyes seem to protrude from his face.

Now, Dick knew that Jesus had said, "They shall lay hands on the sick and they shall recover," but this was the first time such a responsibility had been thrust on him. Dick and his sister laid hands on the boy and prayed as earnestly as they knew how. Nothing apparently happened, and they went back to the church.

Before the week was out, they learned that the boy was up and eating. He recovered completely, and when World War II came, he enlisted and served in the army to the end of the war.

That experience was burned into Dick's memory; how, with fear and trembling, they went to do the Lord's bidding, yet proved the words of Jesus, "Go... and I will be with you."

God did it again in what we shall call, "The Case of the Crushed Skull."

In 1929, there was a terrible motor accident in which two young men were critically injured. In the small town of Bracebridge, it is probable that everyone heard about it. They had been drinking and lost control of the car. It had run off the road, into a steep rock-cut, and the car was smashed beyond repair. On impact, they had been thrown out of the car and onto the rocks. One of them had his skull crushed. His name was Carman.

The doctor told his parents that he would likely die, but that if he did live, he would be a "vegetable" because the brain damage was so extensive. He had been in a coma for several days in the hospital.

The pastor was also janitor, coal carrier, and doorman in those days. Dick went early to the hall where the meetings were held. When he arrived, a lady was walking to and fro in front of the door, weeping. It was the mother of the more seriously injured boy.

She knew the Bombay family and knew they were members of the local Pentecostal church, although she had never attended. She asked Dick if he had heard about the injury to her son, Carman. He replied that he had heard about it and asked her to come in to the prayer meeting and join with the congregation in prayer. She was distraught and could not, since she had to go back to the hospital where she had been almost continuously sitting at her son's bedside. She begged that they would pray for him, for she knew he was not saved and ready to meet God. People were much more conscious of God and the need to be "right with God" in those days. Dick promised that they would pray, and she hurried away.

All the people in the meeting, including George Bombay, did pray that God would heal Carman and save him.

The following Sunday, the mother was in church. When testimony time came, this is what she said: "When I told Dick Bombay about Carman and he promised that you people would pray for him, I went back to the hospital to sit by him." She continued, "Carman was still unconscious, but after a short time he began to stir. Then he opened his eyes and looked at me." She tried to control her voice as she went on, "I could see that he knew me. Then he spoke, and the first words he said were, 'George Bombay is praying for me.'" Delight came to her eyes as she concluded, "I want to thank you all for praying. The doctor says Carman will live, though he may not be normal. Will you still pray that his mind will be all right?"

They assured her they would continue to pray, and they did. Carman continued to recover. The only evidence of his head injury was a tendency to have a nervous laugh each time he spoke. In time, that too disappeared.

The whole family came to the Lord and was filled with the Spirit. Later, Carman married a girl from the church and, in time, became a deacon. They have served God together for years.

About the same time (1929), while Dick was still working sixty hours a week at the factory, he was asked by one of his fellow workers, Bill Ellis, to come and pray for his wife. She was a bedridden cripple and had been totally immobile for some years. Because of the sixty-hour work week, together with his responsibilities on the weekends and evenings in the church, Dick had very little free time to visit. The only time he had was Sunday afternoon. So he told Bill he would come to their house that following Sunday.

Bill's wife was curled up in bed with claw-like hands sticking out on the coverlet. She was very weak and could just barely talk. Of course, she had done no housework for a long time.

Dick asked Bill if he would pray with him for his wife, but Bill just looked embarrassed; he was no praying man. His thirteen-year-old daughter volunteered, "I know how to pray. I go to the Salvation Army Sunday School!" So, together, they prayed.

Bill and his family lived in a company house which could be seen through the windows of the tannery where Dick and Bill worked. Monday morning was a stormy winter day, such as Muskoka often gets in wintertime. Dick went to work as usual. A little later, Bill came to him and led him to a window which looked out over Bill's backyard. There was a woman hanging clothes out on the line. It was Mrs. Bill Ellis!

Bill said to Dick, "Nothing was changed yesterday when you prayed for her. But this morning, she got up, got our breakfast, and began to do the laundry. She washed it all by hand on a washboard, and there she is, hanging out the clothes." By this time there was a break in Bill's voice, and both Bill and Dick were weeping... with tears of joy.

Bill and his family began to come to church. All the family got saved, and later, Mrs. Ellis bore another child. "Jesus Christ came into the world to save sinners."

One Sunday evening during the opening prayer, Dick heard a slight commotion and a voice lifting up in praise, then suddenly it broke out in other tongues. God had baptized Mrs. Ellis with the Holy Ghost right where she stood, with her baby in her arms, and her family all around her.

In rain and shine, blizzard and frost, that family went faithfully to church as long as Dick was pastor, and for as long as he had any knowledge of them.

Dick recalled this incident when he was in Bangkok, Thailand, as a missionary many years later and wrote it down in 1974. He looked back with wonder and thanksgiving at what he saw God do. He gloried in the Name of Jesus who said, "These signs shall follow them that believe... they shall lay hands on the sick, they shall recover." This scriptural truth seemed to follow Dick wherever he went in ministry.

7

Life Takes a New Turn

Plans have a tendency to change without notice when you are involved in Christian ministry.

Dick had just returned to Bracebridge from an extended series of meetings in Michigan and New York states when he happened to meet a brother in Christ who was a commercial traveller. He was on his way south from North Bay, a railway town in Northern Ontario.

He told Dick about two ladies who met regularly for prayer and wanted to see an assembly or church opened. They had rented the lower half of a house in North Bay, but had no preacher. He wanted to know if Dick would be willing to go for two weeks of meetings to help them. The meetings were held in the parlour.

Dick went for two weeks starting on July 3, 1930, and didn't leave again until April, 1934, staying for three and a half years.

They were exciting years of steady growth. It was a time of great revival in spite of the Great Depression, which didn't help much in opening new churches. It didn't hinder either!

By 1931, they had moved from their "parlour church" to a little unpainted clapboard church which had housed an Italian congregation which had dwindled to non-existence. It sat on the rear of a house lot, which overlooked the bank of a creek. The creek was, in fact, an open sewer which ran through the east end of North Bay. The church was heated by a wood stove.

It was during this time of ministry in North Bay that Dick, in January 1931, received his first official credentials: "Recognition of Ministry" by the Pentecostal Assemblies of Canada. Two years later, he received full ordination in London, Ontario, on September 10, 1934, six days after his twenty-fourth birthday.

Life Can Be Tough

A nineteen-year-old pastor, with no denominational affiliation, with a past history of heart and thyroid problems with all the weakening side affects, faced a tough assignment. Although he had been healed of the thyroid, goitre, and heart problems, and had since developed unusual strength by working in the tanneries in Huntsville and Bracebridge, not to mention the rock quarry, Dick was still just a nineteen-year-old.

Times were tough. Money was scarce. At times, it seemed there were only a few coins circulating in the whole of North Bay, and barter was as common as purchase.

The winters were cold, and the snow was deep in those early days of the Depression. It seemed that both nature and the elements were bent on pushing back the encroachments of men. And, of course, the church was imbedded in this milieu.

Heating the rooms Dick stayed in, and more important to him, the old building which was the "church" was a challenge.

Then they learned that the city of North Bay had struck a deal with the government about Crown Lands. It would allow those on "relief" to cut fuel from the forests, seventeen miles north of the city. That was all well and good, but how in creation would they get there and back, and how would they pay the fifty cents levy per cord?

It was an impasse for all concerned, until finally the city of North Bay took on the burden of the cost of the wood, "on the stump." That simply meant that the large trees had to be cut off the stump, cut into stove length pieces, and piled. It also included the side-duty of cutting out the brush in the immediate area.

All of this had to be done in waist-deep snow and below-zero weather. The city then provided open trucks to take the workers to the woods each day, and then haul the wood back to North Bay.

Dick recruited three men to help him. For two days they rode in the freezing cold in the open trucks, carried their own lunches, and cut wood... and cut wood... and cut wood. Two of the men dropped out after two days. That left Dick and Ted Duggard to carry on.

Ted was a strong man and very willing, but he knew very little about the bush. He didn't know how to fell a tree in the right direction, or how to pull on a long cross-cut saw. He wasn't even adept at swinging an axe. This was the pre-chain-saw days!

Both men were exhausted by the end of the day, short as the days were. Darkness descended at 4:00 p.m., and then they had an hour's ride home in the icy cold on the back of the truck. But Ted stuck with Dick, and for several weeks they cut, split, and piled the wood near the roads which had been cleared into the woods.

Some men were cutting only enough wood for their own homes for the rest of the winter. Dick and Ted were doing that, too, but also for the church. Dick knew that green wood was not the best, but that's all that was immediately available as they cut. But Dick was a forward thinker. He was looking ahead to the next winter as well, and to good, well-dried maple hardwood which would burn more easily, and certainly more cleanly.

When March came, the frozen roads began to break up. Yet there was a lot of wood still to be gathered up for hauling down to the city. Wading through waist-high snow, carrying one or two blocks of wood at a time, was even worse than hauling on a cross-cut saw all day.

When the hauling began in earnest, they rode home with the truck driver to show him where to dump the wood. Two loads a day would be dumped in Dick's driveway. But that was not the end of it. This had to be cleared and stacked to make room for the two loads coming the next day. Dick went to bed totally wiped out, only to rise early the next morning to catch the truck.

The wood had been split, but the "large splits" had to be split again in order to fit into the stoves. For several months following, Dick split wood. He had no car at the time, so he filled the garage, and piled it under the stairs leading up to his apartment. Then, of course, it had to be carried up those same stairs when it was needed, armful by armful. The same for the church.

It wouldn't have been so bad, nor the need for such quantities so demanding, had there been modern insulation as we know it.

All the while this full-time job was going on, he was continuing his preaching, his visitation, and all the work of a pastor. He kept in mind the exhortation from Scripture, "Whatever you do, do unto the glory of God." It kept him warm at home, and the people warm at church, but even for a young fellow, it was tough stuff. Although it didn't seem to hurt him. For being a relatively small man, he had enormous strength well into his old age.

A lady evangelist from an internationally-known organization had been invited to preach, but after one week of meetings with no results, she announced she was leaving. Before she left, she lectured Dick at length about the poor building and its awful location. She went on to point out, too, that a little bit of advertising wouldn't have hurt. She blamed the poor meetings and lack of results on these combined factors. There was a good deal of truth in what she said.

Just after this, Dick's mother wrote that his father was sick; if Dick wanted to see him again, he had better come home. Dick went home, and within a few days, his father died. Dick remained for the funeral and long enough to help his mother clear up the few affairs.

The day of the funeral was a bitterly cold -42ºF. Dick got a severe case of the flu, but returned to his responsibilities in the church in North Bay. It was the only time he can remember that he ever wanted to "throw in the towel" and just simply close down the meetings. However, he carried on the "special meetings" with himself as the evangelist, though he was so sick he could hardly talk.

There was no one to call on to help him, and the church had no money to pay anyone to come. He got out of bed Sunday morning and conducted the service. He spent the afternoon in bed, but got up again for the evening service. Every moment was a struggle. His fondest wish was to close the service and crawl back into bed.

He recalls, "I don't think I preached much of a sermon. The people were very patient, for they knew how sick I was, so I struggled on as best I could. I was about to give up and dismiss the meeting when, suddenly from heaven, the Holy Ghost came upon me. Not only was I anointed to preach, but I was instantly healed. Best of all, the Holy Ghost fell on all those that heard the Word. There was no need to invite them to come to the place of prayer. It was spontaneous; everyone came. We spent glorious hours in the presence of God."

In the wee hours of Monday morning, still in church, Dick asked the people what they wanted to do. It was agreed that they should come back Monday evening. They did, and what a meeting with God they had!

This continued for two weeks, one night at a time. The crowds increased, and people brought their own chairs. No advertising was necessary. Many were saved and filled with the Spirit. Others were healed miraculously.

As a result, they had to get a larger place in the middle of town. Then that building became so crowded, they began to rent the Masonic Temple for their Sunday meetings. God doesn't need advertising!

Dick often said, "Just give Him a chance, then give Him the glory!"

In July of 1930, back when that man and the two ladies invited him to go to North Bay for two weeks of meetings, he felt he could do it, even though no financial support was offered. Dick had recently preached a series of youth meeting in the U.S.A. and, as a result, had about sixty-five dollars in his pocket. Since they were providing no financial support, this money soon ran out.

For the next eighteen months, he barely subsisted. He often had little or nothing to eat. The result was a case of malnutrition.

At one point, all he had was a box of Shredded Wheat and some milk tickets. He lived on that for four days.

Then he decided to talk to the Lord, and he told Him he was really tired of that diet. He later said of this experience, "I should have told Him sooner!" That very day a letter was dropped in his mail slot. In part, it read, "While I was praying, the Lord spoke to me that I should send you five dollars. I told the Lord I didn't know where you were. The Lord told me to send it to North Bay, and I hope this reaches you." No address, just North Bay.

He got it, and he thanked God for it, taking immediate action.

Since it was about noon hour, it didn't take him long to get across the street and settled into a chair in the restaurant. He filled up! In those days, you could buy a substantial meal for twenty-five cents, including a beverage and dessert. He had the works! It was the first full meal he had had in many weeks.

Dick summarized this divine provision in this way, "Thank

the Lord for Sister Field who had been a member of the congregation back in Bracebridge. She had returned to the old family homestead and developed a resort on Rebecca Lake. And thank God He knew where she was, spoke to her as she prayed, and He knew my address, too!"

In 1932, halfway through his first time pastoring in North Bay, Dick had some visitors. They were a disreputable looking trio as they stood at his door. After Dick looked at them for a while, he recognized them. They were fellows he had gone to school with in Bracebridge. One of them had been in the same Sunday School class only a few years before.

Like so many other youths, they had "hit the road," looking for employment, doing anything, anywhere, just trying to survive the Depression. They were on their way north, looking for work in the mines.

Dick lived in rooms above the hall. They refused to let him give up his own bed for any of them, so he let them spread out their blankets on the floor.

Before going to sleep, they all reminisced about their boyhood. All of them had nicknames, but two of them were unusual. McRuer Loshaw was called Inky, because he was part Indian and very dark. Randall Davey was the son of a Holiness preacher and was called Two Hammer Handles. They never could figure out how he came to carry that designation! Johnny Mason was the third, just plain Johnny.

Dick gave them breakfast the next morning, and as they were about to leave, they said they had no money. They rather shamefacedly asked if he could spare a couple of dollars so that they could be sure to eat while they were on the road. Dick had two dollars, which was a week's pay at that time, and he gave it to them. After all, Dick had known hunger – and would know it again!

Nothing more from those three friends. The event was forgotten. It was not that unusual in those days. Hungry travellers came through, and people fed them. It's just that he happened to know these three.

In the meantime, Dick had met the young lady he was to marry, Olive Sternall, daughter of a pastor in Pembroke, Ontario. Plans were going ahead well, and they were looking forward to life and ministry together.

In 1935, more than two years later, Dick was on his way to Stratford, where his bride-to-be now lived, to get married. He stopped at home in Bracebridge to see his mother and sister Dorothy, who still lived there. While he was walking down the street with his mind on his impending marriage, he met Johnny Mason, although he didn't recognize Johnny immediately.

He was wearing a patch over one eye. Apparently a splinter had gone into his eye at a saw mill, and the eye was so badly damaged, it had to be removed.

He had been given quite a settlement in cash from the Workman's Compensation Board, and also a small pension for as long as he lived. After passing the time of day, catching up on all the news, they parted. As Dick walked away, Johnny suddenly called out, "Hey, Dick!" and came toward him. Dick wondered what Johnny wanted.

He reminded Dick of the time he had provided a place to sleep, breakfast, and the little bit of cash to help the three of them get by. He said he wanted to repay the "loan." Dick told him he didn't owe him anything, that it was a gift, not a loan. Dick was like that all his life. He never lent. He always gave.

After all, doesn't the Bible say in Matthew 5:42,

> "Give to him who asks you, and from him who wants to borrow from you do not turn away."

But Johnny insisted. He must have been carrying all his "compensation" money with him, for he pulled out a wad of money larger than Dick had ever seen. There were twenties on the outside of the roll of bills. He peeled off a couple and insisted that Dick take them. That was a lot of money in those days!

Again, Dick told him that he had not lent him the money, but that he had given it. "Well," Johnny said, "I'm not repaying a loan then, I'm giving you this for your wedding."

That's how Dick was able to get a brand new tailor-made suit for his wedding. It was an auspicious beginning for this preacher and his bride in their first days of life and ministry together. It was a lot better than being married in his somewhat raggy old blue serge suit, well worn, and tight around the middle!

Does this sound anything like Ecclesiastes 11:1?

Cast your bread upon the waters, for you will find it after many days... buttered (Dick's Translation).

They would often have visitors come to "see what was happening" in the Pentecostal meetings in North Bay. At times, the visitors were just as interesting as Pentecostals were considered to be.

An elderly, dignified lady came in one day in 1931. She brought along a friend for company, and they sat through the meeting. The friend got saved and filled with the Holy Spirit in one meeting, but the dignified lady remained coolly aloof, although she continued to attend with her friend.

There was no prayer room in the church, so they gathered around the altar for prayer. It was right there at the front of the church where many prayed through their problems, were saved, and were filled with the Spirit. There was much joy and blessing. All the while, this lady sat at the back of the little one-roomed church, waiting for her friend.

One evening, "Pastor Dick" left the altar area and went to the back where she sat waiting. He asked her if she would like to come forward and pray. She looked him straight in the eye and said very haughtily, "Mr. Bombay, I think you are all crazy!"

Dick was somewhat taken aback, but replied, "Keep coming."
She did.

Some time later, she followed her friend forward and knelt to pray. Dick learned later that, being a good Baptist, and therefore very Bible-oriented, she had begun to search the Scriptures. She had become persuaded that she was seeing a re-enactment of events she read in the Book of Acts.

As she prayed, she hesitantly raised her hands as she saw others doing. Shortly after, she slowly fell sideways to the floor, with her hands still extended above her head. Just as gently as she had fallen to the floor, she gently began to speak in other tongues as the Spirit gave her utterance. Her face shone.

Then she began to prophesy of the glory of the coming of the Lord. Suddenly she began to sing a song Dick had not heard since childhood:

"Oh, the crowning day is coming by and by,
When the Lord descends in glory and power from on high.
What a glorious sight will gladden every waiting watchful eye,
In the crowning day that's coming by and by."

Then she described the vision she had seen which had caused her to sing. Her joy was boundless and inexpressible. No one could doubt she had seen the glory of God.

She became "one of them" and soon led her sister and a nephew and his family to the same glorious experience.

When Dick left North Bay, there were sixty-five adult members, saved and filled with the Holy Spirit. In those days, that was considered large for a Pentecostal church.

8

Progress in North Bay

A sweet little old lady used to have to walk past the Pentecostal church on her way to her own. This particular day she was a little bit late and still had several blocks to walk, and since the bells of her church were already ringing the beginning of the service, she decided to go into the little Pentecostal church in North Bay.

In her younger years, she had been a faithful member of the Holiness church down east, but for some years she had been away from following the Lord. She told Dick Bombay later that when she came into the church that first time, where she sat in a seat at the back, she had repented and opened her heart to the Lord again. God restored to her the joy of His salvation, and she lived a joyful life in Him.

Testimony services were always a part of the services when Dick pastored, and one day this little lady got up to give a testimony. She thanked God that He had saved her, sanctified her, and baptized her with the Holy Ghost. At this point, Dick said, audibly, "Praise God!" She emphasized again that she had been baptized by the Holy Ghost, and again Dick audibly praised God with her.

At the close of the meeting, she came to Dick and said, "Brother Bombay, I AM baptized with the Holy Ghost." Again Dick said, "Well, praise God for that!"

She told him later that she thought he was mocking her, for she knew what the Pentecostals meant when they talked about the baptism in the Holy Ghost. It should be noted here that Dick never ever contradicted people when they told him they were baptized in the Holy Spirit. The most he would suggest was that they "stick around."

About that time, a very worldly and obviously sinful young woman was saved. The change in her lifestyle and appearance was quite remarkable and dramatic. She began to seek God earnestly for the baptism in the Holy Spirit. She was prostrated by the Spirit before the altar one evening, and soon began to speak in other tongues and prophesy. She talked about the coming of the Lord Jesus, and her face shone like an angel. The older lady stood watching.

After some time, she plucked at Dick's sleeve and said, "I haven't got THAT!" She was very distressed and shaken by what she had seen and heard. Dick simply replied, "Well, if you ask the Heavenly Father for the Holy Ghost, He will give you the gift."

She knelt right there and began to pray. In a few moments, she opened her mouth to pray out loud, and suddenly, she too "began to speak in other tongues as the Spirit gave her utterance." She gave forth a beautiful exhortation to worship and also spoke of the glory of the coming of the Lord.

When she got up from her knees, she went around hugging all the sisters in the church and shaking hands with all the brothers, exclaiming, "I never had THIS before, I never had THIS before!"

She became as a mother to Dick, and when he needed a lift or encouragement, he would visit her. He always came away blessed. Every church needs a "mother" who can minister to a young preacher.

It was while in North Bay that Dick became acquainted with, and eventually into fellowship with, the Pentecostal Assemblies of Canada. Rev. R.E. Sternall, pastor of the P.A.O.C. church in Pembroke, was passing through North Bay. Rev. Sternall was on his way to Warren, a small village west of North Bay, and had to change trains in town. Having heard there was an assembly in town, he found his way to the church. Dick lived alone in rooms at the back of the church.

He had heard about the Pentecostal Assemblies of Canada and, in fact, had been in one of their meetings in Brantford. Rev. R.E. Sternall talked until he had to leave for Warren, but said he would call in on his way back to Pembroke. R.E. Sternall was one of the seven Founding Charter Members of the Pentecostal Assemblies of Canada in 1917.

Some weeks later, he came back. They talked for several hours, and many of Dick's questions were answered. Pastor Sternall asked if Dick might be interested in attending the upcoming District Conference. Dick also remembered, from a former visit to Brantford, that Pastor Sternall had four daughters.

He arranged for Dick to meet Rev. George Atkinson at the Bombay home in Bracebridge. They went together to the District Conference in London. Dick was recommended for and received his first official standing as a preacher of the gospel. It was "The Licence to Preach."

He was interviewed by senior ministers regarding his beliefs and practices, and Dick, not being a forward type of person but wanting to know, asked a few questions of his own. Though he had no formal Bible training, he found that his own studies of the

Scriptures led him to the same doctrinal position and the same practices as those of the P.A.O.C.

When he returned to North Bay, Dick first discussed this new development with the committee which oversaw the affairs of the church. Eventually, they discussed it with the whole membership and proposed that the assembly join the P.A.O.C. They could all see the value in doing so, particularly because it opened the way for the assembly to receive proven ministry from them.

One of the strongest factors in persuading Dick that it was a wise decision was what he had seen and heard in some of the independent assemblies where he had preached as an evangelist. Some of their practices, and even some of their doctrines, made him wary. There seemed to be little or no discipline or accountability in their churches or among their members.

When he learned why some of them were independent, it frightened him. He felt that he wanted to belong to a body that maintained biblical doctrine and discipline among its ministry. The North Bay assembly voted itself into affiliation with the P.A.O.C.

Dick never had cause to regret joining the P.A.O.C. In this fellowship, he received wise counsel and wide opportunities for service to the Lord – in Canada and in many other countries around the world. He held many elected offices, starting in 1947, including District Sunday School Director, Presbyter, Secretary-Treasurer of the District, Assistant and then Superintendent of the District of Eastern Ontario and Quebec, Assistant General Superintendent of Canada, as well as being a member of countless committees with both District and General Executives.

But it didn't all happen overnight!

9

Signs and Wonders

It seemed wherever Dick went, his ministry was followed with signs and wonders. Had he been that kind of man, he could have developed his own "healing ministry," but he did not. He felt this should be the norm for any Pentecostal pastor.

Two young ladies accepted the Lord at one of the Saturday night street meetings in North Bay. Eventually, they brought their mother and a number of their brothers and sisters to the church, and they also were saved. The father, Mr. Duggard, refused to come and became very angry with his family for attending the church. He was a former Welsh coal-miner, but had brought the family to Canada for a better life and to provide future opportunities for his sons and daughters.

Dick Bombay had tried to talk with him, but was always met with great bitterness and an unreserved opinion of ALL Christians.

Dick left North Bay, and the man was still impenitent.

Three years later, Dick was called back to North Bay for a second term as pastor. Mr. Duggard, in the meantime, had suffered a slight stroke, but it was enough to disable him, and he was unable to return to work. As a result, the family moved out into the country where they lived in a large farmhouse. By this time, the two older sisters had married and were living elsewhere.

One winter day, Rev. Bombay took a young man, Glen, from the church and walked the five miles into the country to visit the Duggard family. Mr. Duggard was very ungracious, and as the visit proceeded, he worked himself into a rage. He seemed like a mad creature as he told the visitors that a young man from the church had seduced his eldest daughter (who was now married). Dick had not known anything about this, since he had been pastoring elsewhere for that period of three years. Yet the father laid all the blame on the church and on Dick. He apparently used this constantly to rail against his wife and children who still faithfully attended the church.

At one point in his rage, he said he would forbid his wife and children to attend church any more, and then angrily told Dick and Glen to leave the house and never come back.

Suddenly, the wife appeared from the kitchen, threw herself on her knees and began to pray earnestly that God would change her husband's mind and be merciful to the children. This only angered him more and, again, Dick and Glen were ordered from the house.

Dick asked if he could pray before they left, and very grudgingly Mr. Duggard consented. That was the one time in his life that Dick "prayed the Gospel." He, in fact, preached a mini-sermon and warned of the results of rejecting the Gospel.

Then Dick went to where Mr. Duggard sat, took his reluctant hand to say farewell, and said, "Mr. Duggard, you have ordered us from your house which is your right. You will not come to church, nor will you let your family, so I will NEVER see you again, in this world or in the next. Goodbye."

They left, and all they could do was pray.

To their great surprise, the very next Sunday morning, in came Mr. Duggard with his wife and all the children. That very day he repented, and surrendered to the Lord. What a change when God came into his life! His wife and children crowded around him and clung to him, and that told the story better than words.

When the time came for him to be baptized, his physical condition had deteriorated, and he could scarcely walk. Two men carried him and lifted him over the front of the baptistery into Dick's arms. He held Mr. Duggard as he would have held a little child, and they went down into the water together.

The whole church knew the situation by now, and they wept openly for the joy of a family united in Christ. But the family! They could hardly contain themselves. In the home, Mr. Duggard became a loving father and husband. There was daily prayer and Bible reading together in that home as long as he lived.

His brother-in-law, also a former coal-miner, was saved soon after, and the two families were quite a sight as they sat together in church worshiping God.

"If any man be in Christ, He is a new creature."

She Put Everyone Off Key!

Mrs. Jennie Dame was one of the two women who had invited young Dick to come to North Bay in 1930 for that series of evangelistic meetings. From a short visit, it turned into a three-and-a-half-year term as pastor of the church. God gave them a great awakening. The few saints were revived, and many new folk were saved, healed, and filled with the Holy Spirit. During that time, Jennie Dame was a good and constant helper.

One day she told Dick, "While I was praying, the Lord gave me a beautiful psalm, and I wonder what I should do about it?" In a way, this was almost amusing, since Jennie could not even carry a tune. She would sing along with the church, but it was in such a pitiful monotone that those sitting near her could not sing. She would "throw them off key," as one member said.

However, Dick was also aware of the fact that Paul wrote under the inspiration of the Spirit, and in 1 Corinthians 14:26, wrote: "How is it then, brethren, when you come together, every one of you hath a psalm...?" But he was still reluctant to let her get up and embarrass herself. So, it was with very definite misgivings that he agreed, at the next opportunity, that she should sing her psalm in the assembly.

The next Sunday, her opportunity came. Dick opened the meeting for testimonies, and, although she was not the first to stand, she finally did. She said, "Brothers and sisters, God has given me a beautiful psalm, and I would like to sing it." There was a startled silence, then a few smiles, and others could not hide their total disbelief. EVERYONE knew Jennie could not sing. And she was as aware as everyone else of the fact that she could not sing. Her face was pale as she lifted her face, then her voice, and began. After all, she was singing to the Lord.

It was at the same time shocking and amazing. Without once faltering in her words, music poured out in a soaring and beautiful cadence which none in that crowd could ever have duplicated. She was carried out of herself and seemed to be tuned in with the choir of heaven. The theme of her song was "The Glories of Jesus."

Incredulous looks on the faces of the congregation slowly changed to wonder, and a hushed reverence filled the place. She sang on with such beauty that it was clear her spirit was exulting in Jesus her Saviour whom she loved. It was not long, but it exalted the Lord.

As she sat down, there were sobs, and a hushed reverent praise went up to God from the assembly. They knew the Lord Himself was among them. As the testimony meeting continued, there was a strong thread throughout all the testimonies. Each magnified the Lord Jesus. It was an awesome atmosphere!

Dick did not preach. There was no need. Everyone was exhorted, edified, and made glad. It was something like when the woman anointed Jesus' feet, bowing humbly before Him; the fragrance filled the house.

If we do not learn to "teach and admonish one another in psalms and hymns and spiritual songs, singing with grace in our hearts to the Lord," we may come to the place where there is entertainment but no edification in the church.

The Peacemaker

Jennie was a very faithful follower of Christ. She had been saved as a young girl, but wandered away from God and got into a bad marriage. Her husband, though claiming to be a Roman Catholic, was an ungodly and violent man. He owned a fleet of taxis, which seemed legitimate, but he had a few other businesses which were neither clean nor legal.

He opposed Jennie in her church-going. Under no circumstances, and no matter the weather, Jennie was not allowed to use one of her husband's taxis to go to church. Her beatings occurred on a fairly regular basis, and she wore dark glasses to hide the black eyes she often had. Her arms many times showed violent bruises where her husband had beaten her. He told her that if she wanted to eat and buy clothes, she'd have to supply them herself, so she got by on selling cosmetics.

Dick was her pastor, and one day he heard that Jennie's husband was sending some of his henchmen to give him a working over. There seemed to be no reason for this, other than the fact that he pastored the church where Jennie attended.

Young Pastor Bombay felt a strange urge to visit the husband in his home and told Jennie of his intention. She begged and warned Dick not to do so. She knew his threats, and also that he had already put several of his enemies in the hospital. As time passed, Dick felt the urge to visit the man grow stronger, so Jennie suggested the safest time would be at noon, when her husband was home for lunch and it was broad daylight.

When Dick showed up at the door, Jennie once again tried to dissuade him and asked him not to stay. Finally, Jennie went ahead and began to prepare her husband's lunch. She introduced the two men, telling her husband who Dick was. He very courteously asked Dick to stay for lunch, but since Dick had already eaten (if you're going to be beaten on, you might as well have a full stomach!), he declined, although he accepted a cup of coffee while the husband ate.

Dick remembered the sense of awful expectation he felt. The explosion which was expected was delayed for some reason, and the husband chatted on quite amicably. Dick didn't try to convert him, or press any point whatsoever, but simply chatted along with him.

When it appeared the husband was about to leave, Dick excused himself and rose to leave as well. The husband reached out with a friendly hand and shook Dick's hand. The preacher then bid them a good day and left.

Later, Jennie told her pastor the outcome. She had cleared the dishes away and was at the sink washing them, when her husband appeared in the door behind her. He stood there, unmoving for a moment. Jennie expected him to punch her in the back as he had done so often before, but as the tension rose, nothing happened. She finally turned toward him rather fearfully, and not knowing what else to say, she finally asked him what he thought of the preacher. He answered, "Not bad, but isn't he young to be a priest?" She stutteringly told him that he was older than he looked. Dick was twenty-two at the time.

For no apparent reason, the beatings stopped. She no longer had to buy her own food and clothing, and some sort of peace settled into the home. Later on, the husband bought a legitimate business in Swastika, Ontario, and she worked with him in the business. Shortly after that, he was saved.

Many years later, when her husband died, Jennie moved back to her own hometown, Mactier, Ontario, where she attended the local Pentecostal church. The pastor was Rev. Fred Mott, married to Dick Bombay's daughter Lois.

Incredibly, these many years later, Jennie was still known as a monotone. Couldn't sing worth beans. Fred Mott and Lois, never having heard of Jennie's anointed singing years before, watched and listened as again Jennie broke out in beautiful silver tones as the anointing came upon her there in Mactier. She sang and praised God with a beautiful song of worship. Same reaction, same result. The Mactier congregation was astounded.

The Motts spoke very highly of Jennie and her help to them in Mactier.

Railings

An elderly woman came into the church in North Bay while Dick was pastor there, and she was accepted among the people. No one questioned her, or had any real reason to do so, and she seemed to give a good testimony. The church did hear something about some problems with her former church association, but everything seemed well.

One Sunday, she stood to testify, and what she said was quite acceptable up to a point. Then suddenly she stopped and began to rail on someone without actually naming anyone. Then she broadened her accusations, making them very general, but again without saying anything specific. It was like an ice cold blanket over the meeting.

Quietly, another lady dropped to her knees to pray, but then she fell to the floor between the seats. From this prone position, apparently still in prayer, she answered the offending woman who was still standing, saying, "Sister, you are the one who is guilty of the things of which you accuse others."

The offending woman could not see where the voice had come from, and she came to a sputtering stop. She made her way down the aisle toward the door, shouting, "You are all hypocrites! You are all hypocrites!" slamming the door as she went out.

Dick had never seen anything like this before, or for that matter, since, and it doesn't take much imagination to consider the sense of disturbance that would have gripped the whole congregation.

Silently, Dick breathed up a prayer for wisdom and help. It came swiftly. He said to the people, "The Bible tells us what to do with divisive people. Obviously, this woman has tried to set saint against saint. If she calls you on the phone or comes to your door, tell her that you will not listen to her nor have anything to say to her. Reject her!"

There were nods of assent throughout the congregation, and with great difficulty, the meeting continued. As you can imagine, it was not an easy situation for a twenty-three-year-old pastor to bring back into control.

On Monday morning, this woman called at the door of one of the godly women of the church, Mrs. Young. She was met with a courteous greeting but a firm refusal to let her enter. She went to a second home and received the same reception.

The following Sunday, when Dick saw her there, he decided it would be wise not to have testimonies in this service. He didn't want a repeat performance. The service went along well until Dick looked down and was opening his Bible in preparation for preaching. When he glanced up, she was standing quietly and said, very meekly, "Pastor, may I say a few words?"

Seeing her meek attitude, he consented, but not without some worrisome misgivings. Here is the story, as she told it:

She said, "When I left the church last Sunday I was very angry. I don't know what made me talk the way I did. And when I heard a sister's voice telling me I was the one at fault, it made me even more angry. Monday morning I went to Sister Young's home, and when she opened the door, she told me that the pastor had told the congregation to have nothing to do with me, and she closed the door in my face. I went around the corner to Sister Doran's home and received the same treatment. I was very angry, but as I stood on the street I knew that wherever I went, I would be shut out. I was dumfounded and felt very lonely. Then I said to myself, 'My God, what have I done that they should all turn me away?' I went home, and I have been crying and repenting all week. I have come to ask forgiveness of this church and of you, Pastor, and especially of the lady who rebuked me. I have been a very wicked woman in what I have done. Will you please all forgive me?"

The church was ready to forgive. Dick, still standing in the pulpit, had no time to consult with anyone, but said to her in the presence of the whole church, "Sister, God has forgiven you, and we forgive you in His Name, but I think it best for you and the church if you refrain from any public utterance for a period of time. You may participate in everything but audible prayer and testimony. Do you accept that?" Her response was immediate and humble. "I accept that thankfully, and ask that you pray for me."

She remained in the church and won the confidence of the whole congregation by her humble spirit and manner of life.

Doubtless there would be more peace in God's family if the ministry of the church gave heed to the command that Paul gave in 1 Timothy 5:20, "Those who are sinning rebuke in the presence of all, that the rest also may fear."

Railings are quite fitting in the architecture of a church, but not from the mouths of its members.

Reformed Ruffians

Some time after Dick went to North Bay, he erected a borrowed tent for meetings, and an evangelist came to help. But the evangelist got discouraged and left. His young bride refused to stay in "that awful place," and Dick was left alone to carry on the meetings. He played the parlor organ and led the singing by bobbing his head. Then he preached. The tent was being well filled, and God was doing some wonderful things.

A young man from Brantford, Jack Piper, came north with his mother for a vacation, and he gave what assistance he could, but he had not yet begun to preach. (Some years later, he became brother-in-law to Dick by marrying one of the four Sternall girls, Aleta.)

A gang of ruffians had been molesting the meetings, and one night as he was riding to his rooms with Jack and his mother, Dick felt a sudden compulsion to go back to the tent. Jack stopped the car, let him out, and drove his mother back to their hotel.

When Dick reached the tent, some young fellows were having a wild time. Tent pegs had been pulled, they were swinging from the ropes, and one fellow had climbed to the peak of the tent and, while trying to slide down the canvass, had ripped it from the peak to the eave. Inside, they had upset everything. The organ was overturned, seats were scattered and the place was in shambles.

Before they knew Dick was among them, he had grabbed two of them by their collars. The rest suddenly took off, leaving their two companions in Dick's hands. At first, he told them he was taking them to the police station, and they began to come along quietly. Then they began to beg off, whining and trying to excuse themselves. Dick finally relented, gave them a pretty strong talking-to, and then they returned to the tent.

By then, the rest of the gang had also returned to the tent. Dick walked the two by their collars right into the middle of about twenty fellows, many of them much bigger than himself. They began to get abusive and threaten him. Dick looked at two of the biggest of them and said something very "unpreacher-like": "Come on!"

They could easily have beaten him to a pulp, but something much more than merely temper arose in him, and they all moved back, still surrounding him.

Dick asked them what the people in the tent had done to them to cause them to want to destroy the tent and the meetings. There was a long silence, and none seemed to be able to think of any good reason. Finally, one of the bigger fellows edged forward a bit, and said, "My sister goes to these meetings, and she likes them" (actually, she had been saved). "From now on, we will see that no one bothers you." And they kept their word.

The next night, a new fellow began swinging on a rope, and just as Dick was slipping quietly off the platform to go out to stop him, he saw one of his "new friends" explaining to the rope-swinging fellow what would happen to him if he didn't stop – and stay stopped!

That was the end of their troubles, and during the next while, some of those ruffians were saved and began to serve God. It was out of those meetings that the North Bay Pentecostal Church really began.

10

Dick – The Evangelist

In 1934, Dick ended his first appointment as pastor in North Bay. He was becoming known as an effective evangelist, though he seldom seemed to get very "worked up" in the pulpit as many Pentecostal pastors and evangelists did. He would lead singing with the guitar, or play the trumpet as someone else led the singing.

While he was still in his teens, pastoring in Bracebridge, he preached in various towns and cities, both in Canada and the U.S.A. Often a week of special meetings, which were planned for one or two weeks, would stretch into a month or more. When he left North Bay, at the age of not quite twenty-four, he had a line up of invitations, and from April 1934 through October 1934, Dick preached in many towns.

He was invited by his future father-in-law, Rev. R.E. Sternall, to hold meetings in Stratford, a recently pioneered Pentecostal church. There, he saw a young girl, almost seven years his junior, whom he could not get out of his mind... and heart. He had seen her before during special meetings he held for R.E. Sternall in Pembroke, Ontario. She was a pretty fourteen-year-old at that time. This time she was seventeen, and stunningly beautiful. It was Rev. Sternall's third daughter – and unclaimed.

Olive had fallen in love at once. Dick and Olive began exchanging letters, at a cost of three cents for each stamp. These letters between Olive, at home in Stratford, and Dick, doing evangelism and church planting in Eganville, constituted most of the courtship, although they saw each other occasionally. Dick "arranged" to be "just passing through" from time to time, and it was just a normal thing to "pay a courtesy call" to Rev. Sternall in Stratford where he pastored at that time. Of course, Olive, all starry-eyed, would be close by her dad at those most important "ministerial interchanges."

While he was on the road, preaching in places like New Liskeard, Guelph, Woodstock, Niagara Falls, Buffalo, Sarnia, Lindsay, and Campbellford. There were many people converted to Christ and thoroughly saved. Miracles of healing took place, and the Holy Spirit was moving.

While preaching as an evangelist in Guelph, Ontario, there was a "Testimony Service" on a Sunday morning during the regular service. One innocent little lady, who was too kind to wish anyone any harm, but who was just about one ounce short of a full quart, gave a testimony. She was not even aware of what she said, even when subdued laughter was the response. This is what she said:

"You know the weather has been unusually cold and we had used up all our coal sooner than we expected. Our pension cheques were not due for about a week. We don't like to go into debt, even for a few days. So, at our devotions in the morning, we told our

Heavenly Father all about it; that we didn't have any coal, and the next day we would be cold and the pipes would freeze.

"You know, Daddy gets occasional work at the Anglican and the Catholic cemeteries digging graves. There had been none for some time, but the Lord killed two Catholics, and Daddy was called to dig the graves. Wasn't that just like our Heavenly Father?" she said.

Unmindful of the light laughter that went through the congregation, she continued:

"So Daddy dug the two graves and was paid the same day. We ordered coal right away, and the coal man, who knew us, sent the coal right away that day!"

Most of the congregation was in tears, either from laughter or at the sincerity of her testimony and the earnest explanation of how the Heavenly Father had provided.

Back in the days when Brantford had streetcars, Dick was visiting there as an evangelist. On Sunday morning, an elderly lady gave this testimony, which was verified by her daughter – at least in part....

"My daughter and I had just alighted from the streetcar, but before the streetcar had moved, a young fellow in a car went speeding by. The car caught my coat and spun me right around, and it's only the mercy of God that I'm not in heaven right now!"

Who laughs at such sincerity?

The Rum Runner

Emery Hawke had a good steady job in the railway shops. He should have been satisfied, but he decided that a bit more income and excitement in life was what he wanted. He became self-employed at night on the river between New York and Ontario, at Niagara Falls – as a rum runner, smuggling.

It was well known in that area that beatings, drownings, graft, and murder were the results of that lucrative, but illicit activity.

Emery was in the thick of it, and when he was brought before the courts on a charge of murder, he escaped conviction on a "technicality" or a "pay-off," whichever you choose to believe.

While Dick was in Niagara Falls preaching in an evangelistic meeting, a young man was saved who had regularly worked for the rum runners when they needed their illicit goods to be unloaded and transported after being brought ashore. After being saved, he gave a good testimony and refused to continue his involvement with the rum runners. They concluded that he would inform on them, and so his life was threatened.

Since Dick was the evangelist who had led the young man to the Lord, the rum runners sent out word that they would "get him," too. Being rather naive at that time, Dick merely laughed at their threats against him.

The parsonage was just around the corner from the church, and, since the pastor had already gone home, Dick stoked the fire and locked up. As he walked from the church to the parsonage that night, a big man stepped out from the dark and confronted him. He told Dick his name was Emery Hawke, and that he had been sent to "get him." He towered over Dick and shouted his abuse and threats. It would be dishonest to say that Dick was unafraid, and he has freely admitted that he's not made of the stuff heroes are supposed to be made.

The big man had been drinking, but was far from drunk. In anger, he called the young preacher unmentionable names, accused him of making the young man an informer, and said he was going to kill him. Dick stood completely still, not knowing what else to do. He may have prayed, but he couldn't really remember too well. Fright has a way of blanking out some memories.

The big man drew back his fist to strike Dick, and Dick just stood there, too terrified to move. But instead of striking him, the big man held his arm poised for what seemed a long time. Then his fist dropped to his side. He just looked at Dick for a while, then broke out, "I can't do it, I can't do it!" and he began to cry. He moved toward Dick, threw his arms around him, and stood there crying as hard as any man can cry. Dick was bewildered. He had said nothing at all, he had done nothing, except perhaps feel a bit of a shaking in his knees.

Finally, Dick led him back to the church. There on his knees, Emery poured out his story of blackness and sin. He showed Dick some fearful wounds he had gotten in brawls and scrapes with the law. He had been shot and knifed and beaten. Dick talked to him about Jesus, His love, His power, and His willingness to forgive and save. It was all new to this big lug named Emery Hawke. He had never been to any church, but when he knelt to pray, he wept and prayed, and prayed and wept some more. God broke in upon him. Dick saw his face begin to shine, and it seemed so natural for him to raise his great paws and praise the Lord.

Then, at about 2:00 a.m., he insisted the preacher accompany him to his home, just around the block. Dick must have coffee with him! Dick had nothing to lose but sleep, so he went along.

He knocked on the door, and his wife, from an upper window, told him to take his drunken friend and go away. It took some time for him to convince his wife that he was not drunk, and that Dick was the preacher.

While his wife was making coffee, Emery insisted that Dick see his two children who were in bed, trying to sleep and probably nervous about another bad night with a drunken father. When Emery walked into the children's room and saw the children, he began to weep again. They went back down to the kitchen and the wife looked puzzled and unbelieving. Emery took her in his arms and told her how God had forgiven him. He then asked her to forgive him too, for his mistreatment of her over the years. At last, she finally acknowledged that something had really happened to him. He had never asked her to forgive him for anything in all the years they had lived together. It was that simple fact which convinced her.

It was near 4:00 a.m. when Dick finally got home to the parsonage. The pastor and his family were almost frantic lest Dick had been a victim of more than threats. They could scarcely believe it, but when Emery Hawks appeared in church on Sunday morning, sober, and told what had happened, they were all convinced.

Emery was a changed man. He brought his children to Sunday School, and his teenage son was saved before the meeting concluded.

"The Angel of the Lord encampeth round about them that fear Him, and delivereth them," but He also "saves all who will call upon Him."

Breaking New Ground

The Pentecostal Assembly in Pembroke decided that they should sponsor the pioneering and opening of a church in Eganville, Ontario. Because Dick has been involved in evangelism and the pioneering of several churches, he was asked to take on the challenge. It was 1934 when Dick went to Eganville.

Still a bachelor, he boarded at the McEllicott Hotel. The bed was good enough, but the food left something to be desired.

Occasionally, believers from Pembroke would come and help in the meetings he was trying to start, but most often, he was alone in his efforts. Another preacher, Newell Wendt, joined him at times, often in "street meetings." That's how it all started – "street meetings." Not too popular anymore...

In the little meeting place, Dick played the organ, led the singing from the organ by nodding his head, and even took up the offering, since there were no "regular" members or adherents. Then he did the preaching and praying.

At that time, Dick got sick. Really sick! No doubt the sickness was further aggravated by the less than acceptable food at the

McEllicott Hotel. He developed a serious and painful kidney infection. He described it as "a burning like fire and a rusty discharge, accompanied by a continuous pain."

One night he was awakened by the pain, and realized he was quite fevered. He painfully paced the room, trying to pray, but the pain was so excruciating that he could not concentrate to pray. There was no one he could call, and he had no money to call a doctor. This went on for several hours. Finally, Dick laid his Bible on the bed, knelt beside the bed, and said, "Lord, please give me something on which to rest my faith." He had always found that biblical praying is the best way to pray – and that it works. He was reading through the Psalms when his eyes lighted on Psalm 42:11, and then again on Psalm 43:5 which says:

> *Why are you cast down, O my soul? And why are you disquieted within me? Hope in God; For I shall yet praise Him, The help of my countenance and my God.*

Dick believed that God had directed him to these verses, and he prayed again, thanking God for His assurance and promise. The pain began to ease, so he got back into bed and finally fell asleep.

In the morning, there was no pain whatsoever. The burning was absolutely gone, and there was not a trace of the rusty discharge – then, or ever again. No trace of the problem ever returned. The Scripture came to Dick's mind: "I am the Lord who is healing thee."

Quite often, various ailments would come upon Dick, and he often felt that he could not conduct the services in his church. In a great many cases, he just carried on, and, especially as he preached the Word, healing would come to him and he would leave the service in better shape than when he arrived. He believed throughout his years of preaching that the same anointing for preaching brings the gift of healing. He said, "It may well be that simply obeying God with faith will loose us from many things which afflict us.

Perhaps we 'give in' too soon and too easily! Anyhow, God is faithful, and I am thankful!"

Newel Wendt worked with Dick in helping to establish the church in Eganville. After some time, they established themselves in a hall, with rooms in the back of the building.

After the service one night, Newel was playing the organ and Dick was reading as they enjoyed the last of the heat from the wood stove in the hall. They were about to go back to their rooms when they heard someone suddenly trying desperately to open the door.

Dick, being the nearest to the door, went quickly and opened it. There stood a young farm hand who had been in the meeting. He was so agitated and out of breath from running that he could not speak. When he got his breath and settled down, he told Dick and Newel what had happened.

He had been under deep conviction but had rebelled and left when the meeting was closed. He had walked several miles when he was seized with the thought that if he did not get right with God that night, he would never ever have another chance. He stopped in his tracks, gripped by terror, and raced back to the hall.

He already knew the way of salvation and was soon on his knees with Dick on one side and Newel on the other. He needed no urging. He cried out to God and said that he wouldn't leave this place until God saved him. The same Spirit of God who brought him under conviction now brought the peace and assurance of his salvation

That was the last time they saw him. The farmer who employed him could no longer pay him, and he left town without a goodbye.

Some years later, at a conference, Dick saw that same young man pressing through the crowd to get to him, assuming he might not know who he was. Dick did know! He told Dick that he had enrolled in a P.A.O.C. correspondence course and later was accepted as a minister. He had gone into child evangelism. Many know the man. It was Clarence Aide, a well-known child evangelist who gave his life until retirement to leading especially children to the Lord.

Dick later wondered if the Lord led them to open meetings in Eganville just so that they could bring Clarence Aide to the Lord – who would lead many more to the Lord than Dick himself.

11

An Important Conversion

On June 26, 1935, Dick was involved in one of the most important conversions in his life. It happened at the altar in Stratford, Ontario. Olive Rebecca Sternall had her name converted to Olive Rebecca Bombay. Olive had just turned eighteen the previous December. Dick was soon to be twenty-five.

Dick first met Olive when he went to Pembroke to preach for her father, Rev. R.E. Sternall. Olive was only fourteen, but both beautiful and a devoted Christian. She immediately fell in love with Dick, but, being just fourteen, there was plenty of time to look at the situation, and Dick was almost seven years her senior.

For all his shortcomings, Dick's own father gave him the best advice he'd heard regarding the finding of a wife. "When you want to choose a wife, get acquainted with her mother. If you like what you see, marry the girl." Dick took that advice seriously... and married the girl about four years later, when her father had taken up the duties of pastoring a church in Stratford. Dick's mother-in-law was a wonderful woman in more ways than can be listed.

Many years later, after Dick had tried retirement several time, he wrote this about the woman all five of Dick's children called "Mom."

"The story of my life and ministry would not be complete nor truthful if I failed to include what part my wife, Olive, played in all this. It is true that I spent eight years in ministry before I married. I do not recommend bachelorhood as a way of life.

"Olive never complained about the poverty we shared, but made the most of it, so that with what we got, she was able to feed and clothe the family. I was never reproached in those earlier years for not supplying the needs of home and family as liberally as many others did.

"In all the problems of church life, Olive has been a real help-meet. I did not burden her with all the problems I was faced with, nor did she question what I knew about our people. Consequently, she would greet the people without prejudice and be friendly with them. They all love her, as I do....

"I think our marriage has been as near to ideal as any I have observed, and better than most. For this she is largely responsible.

"Early on, we began to follow a financial plan which is quite simple: 'Pay as you go, and if you can't pay, don't go,' so that when we retired (every time) we 'owed no man anything.'

"Olive cared well for all of our five children. They would be the first to testify of this. (I, Cal, add my "Amen" to this on behalf of David, myself, Ruth, Lois, and Rick.) Though they knew they did not have what most of the children of our churches had, each has told us that they did not feel deprived; they recognized our financial limitations and accepted them. More importantly, they are all serving God in some capacity, as they have been called. We appreciate our children and their children."

Some time before Dad died, he wrote, "Life is winding down for us and we are content. There has not failed one word of all His good promises and we rest in the promise, 'Hath he not said, I will never leave thee nor forsake thee,' so that we may boldly say, 'The Lord is my helper, I will not fear.'"

After their marriage, life moved on.

They moved to Eganville where they began ministry together. They made pretty good music together. Olive played the piano, and Dick could strum a mean guitar or play the trumpet.

Getting a fledgling church started is no easy matter. When Dick and Olive arrived in Eganville, there was an old rented building to be used for meetings. Dick and Newell Wendt had rented that with some help from the Pembroke church. There was no real congregation.

Dick and Olive started together by having many of their meetings right out in the open air, on the street. They would sing together, Dick singing the tenor following Olive's beautiful soprano while Dick strummed the guitar. The singing was interspersed with occasional testimonies by visiting Christians, and some exhortations for people to turn their lives over to God in repentance and faith for the forgiveness of sins.

This was how it all began for Dick and his family more than ten years before in his hometown of Bracebridge. You don't fix something that's not broken!

As autumn approached, so did the early sunsets. They wanted to continue their "meetings," so they moved under a street light. This was something of a novelty – someone out after sunset, singing under a lamp post. It attracted the curious, who watched and listened. Some were merely curious, others seemed more than curious. As the weeks progressed, the curiosity of the town increased – slowly.

But the lamp light with its street preachers attracted more than just people. Bugs and moths of all kinds circled the lamp above their heads. At one point, a moth began to circle lower and lower, until it was circling the heads of Dick and Olive. While Dick held a note with his mouth wide open, the moth discovered a dark hole into which it could dive – and it did, just as Dick drew in a deep breath.

Dick gasped, sucking the moth in further than even the moth had planned. He sputtered, gagged, and coughed trying to dislodge the moth from his throat. As Dick sputtered and heaved, he was only partially successful. One wing came up. The rest of the moth had found its final resting place.

The "meeting" came to an abrupt halt, as Dick, red-faced and coughing, put his guitar in the case, and, as described in Kipling's poem, they "folded their tents and quietly stole away."

But Eganville was not without its successes and rewards. People came to faith in Jesus Christ. As a result, a baptismal service was planned in the Bonnecherre River which flowed through the village. There was a convenient shallow place just below the power dam. A flat field adjoined that area, where the curious of the town came to watch the unusual proceeding – this act of obedience by the converts to follow the Lord's command.

It had not occurred to Dick that none of the candidates for baptism, let alone the townsfolk, had ever seen a Service of Baptism by immersion. He had, of course, instructed the new Christians as to what they and Dick would do... up to a point...!

The first candidate was an older lady. She and Dick waded out to the desired depth, and he asked her to give testimony to her new-found faith in Christ, which she gladly did. Then, as Dick prayed and was about to plunge her beneath the water, she suddenly disappeared, slipping out of his hands. She had simply bent her knees and was crouched under the water where Dick could see her through the pure clean water. She stayed there. Dick grabbed her by an arm and quickly raised her to her feet and whispered the rather important instructions he had neglected to give in advance. They were some distance from shore, so the lady very sedately made her way to shore, and few were the wiser. A whispered instruction to the remaining candidates, and no further complications occurred. None of the townsfolk seemed to be aware of anything unusual.

Dick wondered, as he continued the baptismal service, if the same kind of thing had ever happened to missionaries. To his delight, many years later, his son Cal, who had been a missionary in Uganda, told of a man he was baptizing in a rapid stream on Mount Elgin. The man was carried away by the current, and chased downstream by several pastors, as he calmly lay on his back in the water with his hands sedately folded over his chest.

Olive became pregnant very soon after marriage to Dick. They had been married in an upstairs hall in Stratford where Rev. R.E. Sternall was holding services, and the marriage was performed by Rev. J.H. Blair. Dick and Olive had been invited to look after the church in Hamilton, Ontario, while J.H. Blair concentrated on getting Braeside Pentecostal Camp opened for its first year in 1935.

When Olive was to have her first child, she returned to Stratford, where David Bradford Bombay was born. Olive was there for about three weeks, while Dick held the fort in Eganville.

The Miracle of the Loaf (No Fishes)

Back in 1935, when it was first decided to open a church in Eganville, it was sponsored by the church in Pembroke. The Pembroke church paid the rent of the hall, at $6.00 per month. The rooms for Dick and his wife were over the grocery store.

They were to live off the offerings after all the other church bills were paid. All the folks who came to the services were new and had not yet taken on the responsibility of supporting a minister.

The Depression was still on, and people didn't have much money in any case.

The church had begun to gather good crowds. As many as eighty were attending from town and the country surrounding Eganville. But 1935 was a terrible winter. Storm after storm filled the roads, and people simply could not travel.

It was on a Saturday evening that Dick and Olive found their cupboard had reached a new low: four slices of bread, and not a bit of butter. They had faced almost the same thing several times before this, and the Lord had prompted people to supply their needs. This was different; no people could get to them to supply their need. It was critical! And they had long before decided they would never go in debt for anything.

The daily train came in about 6:00 p.m. carrying the mail. Dick confidently went to the post office expecting something in the mail. It had happened before! Nothing! There was nothing! It seemed that God had not spoken to anyone about them.

Dick turned back home (above the grocery store – oh, those lovely groceries) and fought the blizzard that was raging across the country. He hated to face Olive, who was expecting their first child at that time. He didn't want to admit there was no way to get provisions for the weekend. But, it had to be faced.

Dick told her the bleak news, and, although he knew it was hopeless, he also told Olive he would go back to the post office. Maybe the mail had not been sorted – or something. There must be a letter.

So, Dick put on his fur cap, pulled up the collar of his Ulster, and waded through the storm once again. As he rounded the corner to pass the front of the grocery store, he had his head pulled down against the wind and snow, but could still see groceries through the window – groceries he could buy... if he just had the money.

As he passed the doorway, a man in a great fur coat came out and nearly fell on Dick. He recognized him as a man who attended the church. He paused to tell Dick that he was in a great hurry, since there were several other sleighs going back to Lake Dore, where he lived. They planned to travel together, and to take turns breaking the trail through the snow and drifts. Then he turned, and was gone.

Dick turned back toward the post office, but a moment later, he heard his name called. He turned, and the great fur coat was coming back toward him. The man unbuttoned his coat, then reached for his wallet, explaining all the while that he and his family had been unable to get through the snow to get to church on Sunday. He explained, too, that he had missed the offering.

Out of his wallet he pulled a two-dollar bill and handed it to Dick. Dick did not tell him how close they were to a dinner-less Sunday, but he did thank him. He also fervently thanked God! As soon as the man's back was turned, Dick dashed into the grocery store and loaded up!

When he got home with his arms full of groceries, the first thing Olive asked him was, "Where did you get the groceries?" In the same breath, she asked, "You didn't charge them at the store, did you?" Not too many wives around like that anymore. Dick assured her that they were paid for, and told her how it had come about. Needless to say, they rejoiced again for the watchful care of their Heavenly Father and for the concern of faithful Christians.

There were many times over the years when they could have gone into debt, even to assure their own comfort, but they decided early that their policy would be, "Pay as you go, and when you can't pay, don't go."

When the time came to retire, Dick said, "We owed no man anything," and added, "I don't expect to die a pauper!" And he didn't. In fact, he could have been a millionaire. But that's another story.

12

Cobourg

A church had been begun in Cobourg by an evangelist who thought it better to be called "undenominational" rather than "Pentecostal," even though he was Pentecostal both in experience and affiliation.

He gathered quite a good following, particularly of some of the "Old Country" people who had previously attended "Chapel" at home in England. When asked by the people what organization he belonged to, he would evade by answering, "I belong to Christ!"

While attending a service in a Pentecostal church in a nearby town, two new Christians received the baptism of the Holy Spirit and came back to the Cobourg church "speaking in other tongues" in a prayer meeting. There was an immediate exodus of the "Chapel" folk, and they never came back. The evangelist was charged with deceit for not telling the people that he was, in fact, Pentecostal. The evangelist left Cobourg, too.

In September 1936, Dick was instructed by the District Superintendent to leave the work at Eganville and go to Cobourg. The District Superintendent did not mention the state of affairs in Cobourg. He was simply given a list of names of people "who used to come."

When Dick began to visit them, to "bring back the lost sheep," he was met with "we were deceived!" which, in a sense, was quite true. The people on the list didn't want anything to do with "tongues."

This left only a handful of people with a hall to rent, a house to rent and utilities to pay – but nothing to pay the pastor. They assumed Dick was being supported by some outside source. They knew that the evangelist had been supported by a large church in Toronto.

After six weeks and no income, Dick called the people together to inform them of the situation. Since the rented house was furnished, Dick and Olive were able to sell their own furniture to buy food. First their kitchen suite, then the range. More of their furniture was sold as time went on. Now, whatever brook there was, was dried up completely.

The people agreed that the mid-week offering should go toward Dick and Olive's support, since both Sunday service offerings were needed to pay the ongoing rents and utilities. Dick and Olive helped by moving into even cheaper quarters. The whole while they were in Cobourg, Dick wondered how they survived.

But there was a spinster who cooked in a local institution. From her meagre pay, every Friday, she bought Dick and Olive a large veal rolled roast, which they ate hot the first time, then cold the rest of the week, sometimes with hot gravy. Several of the people brought in vegetables from their gardens. Occasionally, they were invited to people's homes for dinner, and they took advantage of that to "fill up." They stayed in Cobourg until the church was re-established.

David was just about a year old at that time. Cal was expected some time in December 1937.

The Lord blessed and added to the church so that when they left to accept the call back to North Bay, in June of 1937, the church was stabilized. They were followed by Pastor P. Leach, a church was built, meeting in the basement first, then the upper sanctuary, and eventually a new and much larger church was established, which adequately looks after its pastor.

13

Miracle of the Fishes

But No Loaves

In 1940, North Bay was the railway crossroads of the north. Many thousands of people passed through what was then called the "Gateway of the North." People looking for work, for hope, or just for help.

Among them was Gotthilf Souter. His story was not untypical. He was expecting a letter any day from his father in Switzerland. The letter was to contain a lot of money, since his father was a rich man, he said. Could he stay with the pastor until it arrived?

Dick had seen too much hunger and had heard too many proud stories to believe this one any more than the many others. He was one of the more respectable "knights of the road," as they were called in those lean, mean days. He was passably dressed, well spoken, and had a somewhat interesting foreign accent.

Dick and Olive were not very well prepared to entertain strangers, even though they just might be "angels unaware." In fact, after they shared their meager breakfast with him, they were somewhat embarrassed about what they could offer him for dinner!

Then Dick had a bright idea! Lake Nippissing was full of fish and the season had just opened, so Dick asked Gotthilf, "Do you like fish?" His answer was enthusiastic: "There is nothing I like better." Dick wondered if he suspected that the cupboard was bare, or at least very close to it.

They walked down to the lake, across the C.P.R. tracks, down a few streets, and then out onto the government dock. Dick hoped the fish were as hungry as they were. Dick's fishing gear wasn't up to much, but he could at least cast a lure a bit of a distance. He made his first cast and, "bang," Dick pulled in a nice northern pike. It was hard to keep from grinning too much.

Dick made his second cast and, "thud!" Dick set the hook and cranked it in. A nice fat pickerel; the best tasting fresh water fish in Canada was coming home for dinner.

Dad wrote later that he'd never forget the succession of his thoughts. "I'll show our fine Mr. Souter just how good the fishing is in this lake, and just exactly who knows how to catch them." But try as he might, he didn't get another strike that day. He began to feel guilty, and his next thought jumped on to, "Why try to show off when we already have our daily bread?" So they had bread and potatoes and fish that day – and every succeeding day as long as Gotthilf Souter stayed. In fact, that is ALL they had!

There were many very similar situations in those tough days. They learned, as many other preachers did, to "take no anxious thought for tomorrow, your Father knows your needs." Some people complain that they don't like to live "hand to mouth," which simply means having enough for today only. But it's not so bad when you learn that it's from God's hand to your mouth!

Despitefully Used

Pastor Bombay was a visiting pastor, though he found visitation extremely difficult because of his natural shyness. He went to meet with and pray for people in their homes, whether or not they were sick or in need. He always felt that a pastor's duties were as much done outside the church building as inside. So, against his own natural tendencies, he forced himself to do what he knew was right and necessary.

While visiting in the home of one older man, one of the sons, George, happened to be there. Dick mentioned that he had missed George at church recently, supposing he had been on shift work. But to Dick's surprise, George answered in the heat of anger with, "You know right well why I haven't been there!" Dick had no idea what he was talking about.

As it finally turned out, it seems that while the pastor was making the regular church announcements, he mentioned the Wednesday evening prayer meeting. George thought the pastor had gone out of his way to say that the prayer meeting was more important than listening to "Hockey Night in Canada." Dick was supposed to have known that this was George's favourite radio program (this was before TV) and that he had taken the opportunity to shame him publicly. Dick was totally unaware of this, and George, in his angry revelation of these "facts," threatened to "punch his face in." But worse than that, George said he would never come to church again, and neither would his wife and children. He was still in a tirade as Dick left the home.

Olive saw his distress when he got home, and they prayed that the Lord would somehow open up communications again. He was forbidden even to visit the home, or talk to the wife and children. This continued as a burden on their hearts for several weeks, but, behind the scenes, God was at work.

One evening, during the Wednesday prayer meeting, a request was made that the church pray for this same family, because the wife was seriously ill. She was bleeding internally, and the doctor had been unable to control it. She was sinking fast. Dick and Olive had told no one of the threats and anger of the husband. That evening, the church prayed that God would spare her for her family.

Early the next morning, Dick and Olive went to the home, threats and anger notwithstanding. They were met at the door by the husband, George. and when they asked how his wife was, George answered gruffly, "She's a very sick woman." He did not invite them in, so they asked if they might see her. Reluctantly, George opened the door wider, and they followed him into the room where his wife lay unconscious and pale as death. Her pulse was a mere thread. When they spoke to her, the only response was a slight movement of one finger.

As they stood around the bed with the children looking fearfully on, they told George that they had heard how sick she was, and that they had come to pray for her. They knelt, but George just remained standing at the end of the bed.

Their prayer was simple and quite direct. They asked the Lord to graciously spare her for the sake of her husband and children. Again grudgingly, the husband thanked them for coming, and they left saying that they hoped all would be well. This was a Thursday morning.

When Sunday School began the following Sunday morning, in walked George with their four children and Hilda, his wife. Not another thing was ever said about the anger and threats of just a few weeks before.

From that time onward, George, now a humble and grateful man, took his place regularly in the house of God. When his work permitted, he was present on Wednesday evenings at the prayer meeting, as well as all other services.

Some time later, he was elected to the board of the church and served until his death by accident several years later. Dick and George remained good friends for years after Dick left North Bay to go to Oshawa. Hilda, his widow, told Dick how he often reminded the children to "listen to and obey the pastor."

Doubts... and Things

Dick's first sermon is mentioned elsewhere. His conviction when he was first saved at the age of nine, that he would be a preacher, has also been mentioned.

All his life Dick had heard of the very clear and definite "calls" to go into the ministry, which many men have had. Unfortunately, many of those who were "called" have either been mistaken or have returned to secular employment. No such clear "call" had come to Dick, and this fact rose up to haunt him for thirteen years after he began to preach. It was during his second time pastoring the growing church in North Bay that it seemed to come to a climax.

For a period of about six months, he had been tormented with the thought that he was usurping the place of someone who was truly "called." He considered seeking secular employment. He shared his problem with two senior men in the church, and they lovingly assured him that as far as they could see, he was in the right place in the ministry. Yet, the battle continued in his mind, and he contemplated looking for secular employment.

The inner struggle became so great that he was unable to prepare to preach. He would go before the congregation only because he had to. He wondered, for years afterward, how he ever got by. But the church continued to grow, and everyone seemed to be blessed, except himself. Many times he told Olive that he would not go to church, but he always ended up going.

One Sunday evening, he finally determined it would be his last. He was not prepared, and he went into the pulpit terrified. Somehow, he got through the song service, and while he was leading the songs, he thought, "Well, the least I can do is read a Scripture lesson." So he leafed through his Bible searching for anything suitable.

When the time came to preach, he read the portion, tried to say a few words related to it, and then his mind went blank. He stood there speechless. He just stood there, looking out over the crowd. He went numb and couldn't even think what to do next.

He could not recall just how long that lasted. Time seemed to stand still. He couldn't pray. He wasn't even sure if the people knew there was anything unusual happening. He just stood silently. He was, in fact, afraid he would lose his reason.

It might have been somewhat the same as when Samson's strength returned, or when the Spirit set Ezekiel on his feet, but suddenly the Spirit of God came upon him. He began to speak. It poured out of him, quite literally bypassing his own mind. He had no recollection of what he said, but he was certain it was from God for, in a few moments, the people were on their feet coming to the place of prayer. Dick stood there simply dumfounded at what had happened.

From that moment onward, he never doubted God's "call." It was definitely confirmed to him from the Word of God as he read what Paul had said of his own "call": "God counted me faithful putting me into the ministry" (Acts 13).

A Son of Israel

Directly across the street from the church in North Bay, there was an auto parts supply store. It was owned by a man named Friedman, a Jewish refugee who had fled his native Russia.

After Dick made a purchase one day, he was a little apprehensive when Friedman asked, "Does Mr. Pugh still go to your church?" Dick affirmed that he still did. And waited....

Friedman continued, "One day after he began going to your church, he came in here and said he wanted to pay me what he owed. I wasn't aware that he owed me anything. Mr. Pugh admitted to me that he had been "shoplifting" and wanted to pay for what he had stolen."

Dick seemed at a loss for words, and before he could think of any comment, Friedman continued, "You know those Pringle brothers? Well, they did the same thing. While one was dealing with me here at the counter, the other would wander throughout the shop picking up what he wanted while no one was watching. They brought back a lot of the stuff they had stolen, including an entire transmission! What they couldn't return, they paid for. What do you do to them to make them do this?"

Dick told him that he didn't make them do it, but that when God, for Christ's sake, forgave them, God gave them a new nature so that they wanted to make things right with men, as well as with God. The Jew listened respectfully, and Dick went on to tell him what God could do for those who repented and believed.

But it wasn't long before Dick knew where his interests lay. He soon asked, "Does Frank Soule go to your church? I see his father, Wes Soule, going there!" Dick answered, "Yes, Wes Soule and his brother George come to church, but Frank doesn't."

"Well," Friedman said, "I wish he did. He bought a dump truck from me. He still owes me more than $400.00 and he hasn't been in to make payments. He doesn't answer when I send him his account with me. DO YOU THINK YOU CAN GET HIM TO COME TO YOUR CHURCH?"

That seems like a good way to "let your light shine before men that they may see your GOOD WORKS and glorify your Father which is in heaven"!

So, Who Gets the Glory?

In 1932, they had ninety-three chairs which filled the little church in North Bay. Each one was filled every Sunday. Little children sat on laps, and older children had to sit on the altar rail, facing the congregation. People stood in the aisle, and though it was winter, some stood outside throughout the services. There was a spirit of revival, and the crowd had grown steadily. They needed more seating room.

During the Depression, few had jobs and money was scarce, yet everyone was talking about expansion. One of the few employed men offered some money, $125.00 for materials, and suggested they could all pitch in and do the work themselves. Dick felt the Lord was meeting the need, and he brought the matter before the board of the church. He told them about the offer and that he had figured out the $125.00 would pay for all the material they would need. In the dirty thirties, prices were a bit different than today, yet even with those prices, money was hard to come by. But everyone had some muscle to offer.

One man on the board felt that there was something wrong with one man supplying all the money for the materials. He persuaded the others to turn down the proposal. Dick felt frustrated and had to tell the donor that the work was not going ahead. (Dick seriously doubted that he would be quite as submissive to such an attitude in the board in later years.)

The crowd continued to grow, but it was inevitable, when people came and couldn't get in, that they turned away, and some didn't bother to return. The Lord continued to bless, but the impetus had been lost! Tragic in many ways.

At a board meeting, almost a year later, the same man who had opposed enlarging, brought forward an almost identical plan as though it was a new idea. HIS OWN! As he promoted the idea,

Dick became indignant and was about to speak out and let them know that it was the same plan he had proposed less than a year before.

Just then, it was a though a hand was laid on Dick's shoulder, and an inner Voice spoke, "What does it matter who gets the credit as long as the job gets done?" And the job did get done! They were able to seat more than thirty extra people, and still the crowds increased.

Eventually, they had to rent the Masonic Temple for the Sunday services. People came, and the crowds almost doubled. This continued for three months, and then the same reluctant man objected. Dick recalls, as though it was yesterday, the man saying, "I can't see us paying out money every Sunday and leaving our own building empty and dark!" The other men listened to him, and a formal resolution passed disapproving the rental of the Masonic Temple.

They took their meetings back to their little church, but something happened. There was a "settling down" that could not be counteracted. The burden for that church began to lift from Dick's heart. He knew he had done all he could there, so, when a call came from a church in Oshawa, the Lord made it clear to him that he should accept it.

God has only one direction, "FORWARD!" (Exodus 14:15).

Out of that experience, Dick formed a phrase which became a watchword, often voiced, which goes like this: "I don't care who gets the credit, as long as God gets the glory!" He also was able to plant seeds in the minds of the people he worked with in such a way that when a new idea or proposal came up for consideration, the others thought they had actually originated the idea. THAT takes finesse!

14

Oshawa

Dick and Olive moved to Oshawa with their two sons, the oldest, David, and myself, Calvin. We lived above the church in a big cement block building. The church was located right on the busy Highway 2, on a hill. All night, trucks would labour and grind their way up the hill going west.

Some terrible things almost happened there. I (Calvin) went missing. Frantically, Olive search and called. Finally, I was found, sound asleep in the wide gap on a window ledge, between the curtains two storeys above a pile of stones. Mother never seemed to experience too much pressure, or, if she did, she didn't show it to us children.

One night, Mom and Dad had gone for a walk to get an ice cream down the hill at a corner shop. They had left David and me sound asleep. One of us woke up and, between the two of us, we decided that we had been abandoned.

When they came back, there was a crowd in front of the church, right near the curb. David and I had gone down the stairs and outside in our search for Mom and Dad, and finally sat down crying on the curb. We attracted a small gathering just as Mom and Dad approached. Meanwhile, massive trucks were lumbering up the hill just a few feet from our feet. We were taken inside and given a few instructions. Dad, being a preacher, you'd think would have taken advantage of a small crowd and preached the gospel to them. Instead, we got his attention.

We had a beautiful collie dog. It barked a bit, but that's what he was supposed to do. One of the neighbours poisoned it, and we were heartbroken.

Halfway up the stairs to the apartment above the "sanctuary" was a window with a wide sill. I can recall Dad's love for very old cheese. Old cheese stinks. Mom felt the window sill was the best place to keep Dad's gorgonzola. That little window looked out over a graveyard just behind our backyard. That brought many a tremor to our childish young minds and emotions.

That same backyard was the playground for Dave and me and some neighbour kids. Dad would often join us in fights between two snow forts. Snowballs would sometimes collide in mid-flight, and one once lodged in my mouth, almost choking me as I was shouting innocent imprecations against the enemy fort. David and I always took opposite sides, but Dad would join in from both forts. He loved seeing us have fun.

Dad, or, as he was best known by his friends, Dick, had bought a Model A. The canvass over the roof was ripped a bit, but it took him throughout the city to do his pastoral duties, as well as helped him perform his duties as Warden in Oshawa during the Second World War.

Oshawa was called "Motor City" in those days, where General Motors built cars. It was a tough place in many ways, but everyone took pride in the fact that the "Buick" was first built there. R.S. McLaughlin had turned his father's carriage business into a car manufacturing company called General Motors of Canada. The famous "McLaughlin Buick Eight" became a part of the GM family. Most of the congregation worked either directly for GM, or for GM related parts factories. In some ways, it was not a healthy city, but R.S. McLaughlin lived to be 100. He was often called "Mr. Oshawa."

Four Out of Five Died

There were reports of an unidentified epidemic running through the Oshawa General Hospital. Some children had died rather quickly, and a specialist had been called in to try to diagnose the problem and, if possible, help curb the epidemic. He eventually described it as "some virulent fulminating micro-organism" which choked the patient to death. The tremors of fear had begun to spread in the community, and those with family, particularly children in the hospital, lived in terror of what might happen.

Dick received a frantic call from a mother whose child was in the hospital. She brokenly told him, "Our baby is in the hospital, and they don't think he will live. He has this bug that is killing the children!" He had married the young couple some years before, but the home had not been blessed with children. Just shortly before, they had finally adopted this little boy. They deeply loved the child.

Dick immediately left for the hospital where he met the tearful parents. They led him to the isolation ward, wringing their hands in dread. As Dick bent over the little child, he could actually feel how hot the child was from the fever that was consuming him. With every breath, the little body arched in its effort to get air into its lungs. By this time, the mother had become hysterical. Dick quietly asked the father if he could take his wife out to try to calm her. Meanwhile, he stayed with the child, alone.

Dick laid his hand on the little child's head and prayed a very simple prayer for his recovery. There was a short period of continued struggling and writhing for breath, then the body suddenly subsided and lay quite still. For one frightful moment, Dick thought the child had died, but as he looked closely, he saw what appeared to be normal breathing. He touched the little face. It was cool to the touch, and the skin tone had reduced from the deep red to a natural colour. He could hardly believe the remarkable phenomenon he was witnessing. He stayed with the child for quite a while.

He finally went into the corridor and called the parents. Assuming the worst, the mother began to scream, "My baby is dead. My baby is dead!" She clung to her pastor hysterically while he tried to calm her and assure her the baby was alive. He finally led them to the little crib where the baby appeared to be sleeping peacefully.

The local doctor, whom Dick knew, and the specialist had heard the commotion and rushed into the room. They observed the child for some time. They took his pulse. They took his temperature. Eventually, they seemed satisfied, although a little nonplussed.

The doctor turned to Dick and said, "Reverend, what did you do?" He simply told them the truth: he had prayed to God to heal the child. The doctor returned, "Well, it must have been that God heard you, for if this baby lives, he will be the first. We have lost four already!" Others died as well.

This child lived. The parents took him to church a few times, but they were not committed Christians and soon fell away. Shortly after, they moved from Oshawa, and Pastor Bombay lost contact with them.

Humour in a Testimony

Dick always had an unusual sense of humour. It was apparent in the home, in any small gathering of people, and often even in church from the pulpit. But this time, it came from the pew.

Herman did not have much opportunity in life. He couldn't read, so he depended basically on what he saw, heard, and felt. He started drinking quite early in life, and his life began to revolve around drinking and dancing. Finally, he became a weekend drunk. Debauchery led to further debauchery. You probably wouldn't have chosen him as a neighbour.

Then Herman met the Lord Jesus. He became more enthusiastic about the Lord, the house of God, and the people of God, than when he was once dedicated to serving the flesh and the devil. He was completely delivered from alcohol and the worldliness that went with it.

He always sat with his wife to the right of the pulpit, second seat from the front. In a Testimony Service, he would stand to his feet, turn and face the congregation, and always try to glorify the Lord with what he said. One morning, his testimony went like this:

"You all know what the Lord has saved me from. I don't drink and dance like I used to. And I give my testimony among the men I work with. Sometimes they give me a rough time of it.

"This last week, I was telling them again how the Lord saved me and cleaned up my life. One man said, 'Herman, you know you don't drink and smoke because that preacher down at your church won't let you. Why, my preacher comes on down to the Legion Hall and takes a drink with us often.'

"Says I to them, says I, 'No sir, the Lord saved me and I don't want any of that now.' And, says I, 'My preacher wouldn't do such a thing as that!'"

Then Herman swung around to face Dick where he stood behind the pulpit, and said, "Leastwise, as far as I know, he doesn't!" The crowd burst out with laughter, and Dick joined in with them. But Herman looked bewildered. He didn't understand why everyone was laughing.

When the laughter subsided, Dick said, "I can assure you, Herman, that you were right. I don't drink at all." Herman looked a little uncertain for a moment, and then said, "Well, I'm glad to hear THAT!" Another burst of laughter filled the church as Herman sat down.

Herman's life was consistent with his testimony. It was some years later that Dick's phone rang, and he was informed that Herman had taken a very severe heart attack at work, and they had sent him home, not knowing how serious it was. From home, they had called an ambulance to come and take him to the hospital.

When Dick arrived at Herman's home a few minutes later, he was still sitting in a chair in an attempt to make breathing easier. His face was livid and his breathing laboured. He grasped Dick's hand, and said, "Brother Bombay, the pain is awful." Dick began to pray for him, and Herman, between gasps, began to praise God, repeating, "Isn't Jesus wonderful!?"

Those were the last words he said. The ambulance arrived and quickly took him to the hospital. Dick followed in his car, but when they took him out of the ambulance, he was already dead.

Herman died as he lived: praising God!

Should Dick Be an Apostle?

Some people are gullible.

One little old lady, who seemed to enjoy her "Gullibles Travels," became rather enamoured with one of the many places and meetings she frequented. It was her habit to go to whatever church where she heard things were "happening." She was convinced that she had discovered the truly "apostolic" church in a nearby city. She began to spread their literature in the church Dick was pastoring in Oshawa, and she tried her best to convince Dick that he was "too good for the Pentecostal Assemblies of Canada." "No liberty of the spirit, you know!" Of course, Dick didn't know any such thing. But the lady persisted.

She acted as a self-appointed agent to sell Dick's good points to the leaders of this little group, and they seemed quite ready to listen to her. She convinced them that Dick was worthy, and one day she came to him to announce that "they" thought he was qualified to be an "apostle." Dick didn't buy that either. And he didn't become an apostle... then!

Then, along came another teaching, generally called the "latter rain." Hearing the amazing reports, Dick and Olive, along with another minister and his wife, went to Detroit, where apparently authority had been transferred from its birthplace in Saskatchewan.

Ministers from all over Canada and the U.S.A. were gathered. It was like a continual convention, with prayer, singing, preaching, and many professed prophecies. Most of the prophecies predicted that God was going to do a "new thing" which would far outweigh and outshine the Pentecostal outpouring which had begun at the turn of the century. No doubt there were many very honest and earnest people who had come to seek God. Dick was well acquainted with many people he saw there, both laity and ministers. Good people.

One of the first things that came to Dick's attention was the great number of "independents" who were there. They belonged to no organization and were accountable to no one. Were they becoming dissatisfied with their independence?

The next thing he perceived was the existence of a power struggle. Who would become recognized as "The Apostle of the Latter Rain"? He was aware of one who had already manipulated his way and made a bid for the leadership of the P.A.O.C. In this gathering, this same minister appeared to be the "prophet" who was "calling out" those who were to have hands laid on them for the imparting of "gifts." Several had been called out and various "gifts" were bestowed by prophecy.

The third day they were there, they were all kneeling in prayer throughout the sanctuary. Dick heard his name spoken and then repeated. He looked up and was beckoned to the altar area where a group of men stood. When he approached, they began to gather around about him, and the "prophet" said, "Brother Bombay, God has called you to be an apostle, and we will lay hands on you, imparting the gift to you."

Suddenly, a feeling of revulsion came over Dick, and he began to back away. One of the men he knew actually tried to coax him, telling him what a great blessing it would be to his ministry.

Dick looked at him, and said, "No, thank you, I already know what God has called me to be and to do, and I know my ordination. You can add nothing to that and I want no part of this!"

They were shocked. Who ever heard of anyone refusing to become an apostle? Surely this man Dick would be in trouble. They seemed to think the judgement of God would fall on Dick right there on the spot. He turned and went back to his place of prayer.

Where are those men who presumed to "call" men to any ministry? Dick followed their careers through the years. One has been in and out of the ministry for many years, trying to find his place. Another lives like a prince among his few followers. Others have gone down in disappointment and discouragement, and have returned to secular employment.

Jesus asked, "How can ye believe, which receive honour one of another, and seek not the honour that is from GOD ONLY?" And where is the whole "latter rain" movement today? The name itself is almost forgotten.

Meanwhile, another important thing happened in the Bombay family. Dick took my older brother, David, and me out for fish and chips. A most unusual thing. Dad seemed to prolong the meal more than was necessary, but we didn't complain. Time alone with Dad was precious. The big surprise was when we got home, we found that we had a baby sister, Ruth, born that December 7th.

God continued to bless Dick's ministry in Oshawa in many ways. Witnessing the wonderful works of God was a normal experience and expectation. Although he had once been doubtful of his place in the ministry, several things he never doubted: God's Word, and God's power to answer prayer. He had a bit of a reputation for receiving answers to his prayers. He was not the usual stereotype of Pentecostal preachers when it came to ministry, either in the pulpit or in prayer in a private situation. He rarely raised his voice except to be heard by a large crowd.

One day, a woman called Pastor Bombay on the telephone, very apologetically introducing herself and stating her problem. She said:

"You do not know me and we do not attend your church, but we have heard that you pray for the sick. My aunt has had surgery for internal cancer, and she has been sent home to die. Would it be an imposition if I asked you to come and pray for her?"

Of course, Dick went! He discovered, when he arrived at their home, that the lady was a member of one of the old, well-known families in Oshawa, and that many members of the family were professional people. Again, the lady who called apologized for asking someone who was not their own minister to visit. Then she said:

"'Our bread delivery man (and she named him) attends your church. Almost every Monday he has a story to tell of the wonderful things that take place at your church. When Auntie took sick, I asked if he thought you would come and pray for her. He said he was sure you would, and he gave me your telephone number."

The aunt was lying in bed, looking very frail, her skin almost transparent. Pastor Bombay talked for a while, recounting some of the "wonderful works of God" he had known. He then read some faith-building portions of God's Word. Putting the Bible aside, he asked her, "What is it you want God to do for you?" She replied that she kept house for a nephew (who was a dentist) and a niece (a music teacher – the lady who had called Dick) and she wanted to be able to keep house for them again. She told Pastor Bombay that she was seventy-two years of age.

Dick then turned to the niece and asked, "Do you believe God would heal Auntie?" She affirmed that she did believe it. Dick then asked the nurse who was attending Auntie, "Do you believe God can heal her?" She replied that she was a Mormon and that she believed in healing. They all joined in prayer, and Pastor Bombay anointed Auntie with oil and laid his hands on her. After a few more short words, Dick excused himself and left. They thanked him profusely for coming and caring.

Dick heard nothing more from them, and so, several weeks later, being curious, he knocked on their door. The nurse answered the door, and he asked, "How is Auntie?" The nurse turned and said, "Come in and see!"

In the parlor, Auntie lay on a couch, fully dressed. She held out her hand and asked if Dick would forgive her. She always lay down after lunch and was not expecting anyone.

Two weeks later, he called again. This time, the door was answered by Auntie herself. She had a broom in her hand and told him she had just finished "sweeping up." She said she felt well and was able to keep house again.

Then she showed Dick her hands. They were red and scaly, the result of poison ivy, which recurred every summer. Dick took her hands in his and prayed again for healing. The next time Dick called, she held out her hands, saying, "Look! It's all gone!"

She lived to seventy-eight, then peacefully died in her sleep one night.

An interesting incident took place, years later, when Dick's oldest daughter, Ruth, was working as an R.N. on the night shift in Oshawa General Hospital. Auntie's nephew, the dentist, lay dying and was one of her patients. He told her he was afraid to die. Ruth had already witnessed to him, explaining faith in Christ Jesus. She asked if he would like her to pray with him. He was thrilled that she did, for after prayer, he told her, with wonder, that his fear had all gone. He passed peacefully into the presence of God a few days later.

Back before God was put on the shelf by society, some good things happened in the schools. Now... well... think that one through! But when it was still possible, often very remarkable things occurred.

The Ministerial Association of Oshawa was involved in the educational process throughout public and high schools of the city. For many years, Dick was one of those who taught Christian education. There was a prescribed curriculum, and it was taught from October through May every year. However, in grades seven and eight, the ministers were expected to prepare and teach their own lessons.

One day, as Pastor Bombay was leaving the classroom, the teacher, a man of about forty years of age, told him of a particular problem in his class. Apparently, there was considerable pilfering, and at times, some very serious theft. As a result, there was considerable lying as the students were questioned. Everyone denied guilt and any knowledge of the missing articles.

The teacher asked, "Do you think you can do anything about it?"

The good Reverend gave it some thought... and prayed.

Before his next lesson, he leafed through some of the future lessons and found one he thought might lend itself to the situation. He prayerfully prepared the next lesson, asking for the Lord's help and guidance.

Dick was always a very straightforward man. His habit was to avoid beating around the bush and to get to the matter at hand, both clearly and immediately. He was prepared.

When he went in to the next session with that particular class, along with other points, he spoke candidly about stealing and lying. He said, too, that he had learned that such things were happening in this class. He never mentioned that the teacher had been the one who had informed him. As he continued with the class, he noticed something unusual happening among the children.

It was customary to close each session by repeating the Lord's Prayer together. They would bow their heads over their arms which were on the desks. However, this day, instead of launching into the usual prayer, Dick spoke very briefly to the class of the problem again, and then said:

"Girls and boys, I am going to pray, a sentence at a time, in which I will confess the wrongs done. If you wish to repeat them after me, you may do so, but no one is compelled to do so. You also know of other things you have done that are wrong. You will also be given time to confess those things quietly to God."

At first, Dick heard only a few murmured responses, but soon everyone was repeating the prayer. He heard some sobbing too, and when the prayer was finished, he told them that he was going to pray *for* them. Dick glanced at the teacher, and he was facing the window, also sobbing.

After he prayed, everyone remained with their heads bowed, including Dick and the teacher. He wanted to give them time to dry their tears and compose themselves so they would not be embarrassed before one another. He also added a few appropriate remarks which helped.

A few weeks later, the teacher told Dick of the remarkable transformation in his class. No more lying or stealing, and also, no more disciplinary problems.

On Dick's last day with that class that year, the teacher thanked him. But Dick was greatly surprised when one of the boys stood and made a little speech to thank him, saying, "We are going to try to carry out what you have taught us." Then the boy handed Dick a lovely farewell card, signed by every member of the class. It was one of Dick's most cherished memories.

15

Pastoring is Not Always Fun!

One of the church members came to Pastor Bombay one day, and, although surprises were rare to him, this time he was surprised.

As soon as the agitated church member had sat down in the pastor's office, he blurted out, "I have committed adultery with...!" and he named the married woman. "The baby she has just borne is mine. I want to make a clean breast of it, and I am prepared to take whatever punishment I deserve."

She was a wife and the mother of three children, besides the new baby boy. The young husband had already instituted divorce proceedings. All this had taken place and Dick had heard nothing at all about it until this revelation by one of the guilty parties.

He took the matter before the church board, and, since both parties acknowledged their guilt, it was agreed that both parties should be required to cease from all public ministry activity in the church or anywhere else for a period of two years.

By this time, the rumour mills had begun to release the story, and it was thought best, by both the board and the pastor, that he should preach a sermon on "Discipline in the Church."

After the sermon, everyone but the adult members of the congregation would be released from the meeting, and a statement, in which both parties had admitted their guilt and which had been prepared in advance, would be read to the church. I remember that Sunday clearly. I was just a few years too young to stay in the meeting. Many of us met outside inventing all kinds of conjecture. We never did find out what happened until years later.

Both offending parties were in the meeting, and heard and agreed that the facts stated were true. Both parties signed a copy of the statement. Dick then had the congregation bow in prayer, giving an opportunity for the offending parties to leave.

All of this had taken the majority of the congregation by surprise. The whole church sat in silence for some time, and then, throughout the church men and women were heard to be quietly sobbing. Some were crying openly. Others began to cry out to God audibly. When this had subsided, Dick led in prayer, then asked the congregation to do two things.

First, he asked that they continue to pray for the two families involved. Second, he requested they not discuss the matter with family or friends, especially those outside the church family. After all, it was a church matter and had been dealt with properly.

It was the hardest public action Dick ever took. Quite naturally, he was upset for the rest of the day. In fact, he had been so occupied with the affair that he had failed to prepare a sermon for the evening service. He just could not bring his mind to focus on any preparation. Olive remembered that it was probably the most difficult situation he had ever faced in the church.

The next morning, Dick happened to meet the Baptist minister in the post office. Word gets around. He had heard what Dick had done the day before, and he said, "I heard what happened in your church yesterday. I highly commend you for your dealing with the situation... too bad more ministers don't have the courage you had!"

Finally, Dick began reviewing former sermon notes. He found one which was liberally filled with Scriptures and decided, "If I cannot preach, I can at least read enough Scripture to hopefully do someone some good."

That evening service was not easy. It was as equally disturbing and difficult as the most unusual morning service had been. Somehow, he was able to get through the service, preach, read the Scriptures, and almost out of habit, give the altar call. To his astonishment, five adults, whom he had never seen before, responded. They came to the altar in repentance and faith for salvation.

Dick was overflowing with gladness at what God had done, for it brought the whole matter into proper perspective. Dick *knew* that no matter what happened, Jesus Christ was in the midst of His Church. It also proved to him that when things are done according to the will and Word of God, even though in fear and trembling, God Himself will work in and with His people.

Divorce proceedings were halted and then cancelled. There was forgiveness and reconciliation between the young couple. The home of the older couple was also saved. The offenders proved their sincere repentance, and the church board was persuaded to shorten the period of probation considerably. The church also learned to pray for and to forgive the erring.

Dick had been taught by his older brethren, particularly Rev. R.E. McAlister, that in the ministry nothing is settled properly until it is settled according to the Word of God.

He has shown you, O man, what is good. And what does the
Lord require of you but to do justly, to love mercy, and to walk
humbly with your God? (Micah 6:8).

The Indwelling Spirit

Dick had just arrived home from visiting one day, when the telephone rang. It was a friend, Lennox Smith. He quickly told Dick of the fact that the Griffin family had been in a terrible auto accident, and that the whole family had been taken to Oshawa General Hospital. Dick and Rev. George Griffin were very close friends, and Dick was at the hospital within minutes.

Apparently, George and Alma Griffin, together with their two sons, Murray and Donald, and George's parents, were on their way home to Toronto from Cobourg's Lakeshore Pentecostal Camp where they had just closed up their cottage for the winter.

About a mile west of Whitby, a truck had suddenly pulled onto the highway on the wrong side of the road, and a head-on collision resulted. The Griffin car was completely destroyed, thrown off the road, and the whole family rushed to the hospital.

When Dick arrived at emergency no. 1, he found that the boys, Murray and Donald, were badly bruised and dazed, but otherwise whole. Both George and Alma were badly battered, but not seriously injured. George asked about his parents who were in another emergency room, so Dick went there to inquire. It was quite a different story there.

Both Grandfather and Grandmother were on examining tables. It was obvious that Grandmother was seriously injured, since her shoulder had been driven up beside her head. Yet she was conscious and asked Dick, "How is Daddy?" Dick went to the second examining table, and the doctor, whom Dick knew well, shook his head and told him there was no hope at all for Daddy. The side and back of his skull were badly smashed, exposing the brain. He was totally unconscious.

As the doctors continued to examine him, removing bone fragments, Grandfather suddenly began to speak in tongues, lifting his hands from time to time, shouting "Hallelujah!" This rather startled the doctor and continued for some time. The doctor said, "This is most unusual! We often hear cursing and foul language, but this is the first time I've heard an accident victim doing this. Is he some kind of foreigner? He seems to speak another language."

Dick explained briefly that he was a Christian, and that he was filled with the Holy Spirit. He explained that he was "speaking with other tongues as the Spirit gave utterance" (Acts 2:4). He quickly told the doctor that Grandfather was praising and blessing God, and that he was dying the same way he lived. The doctors understood.

The other members of the family eventually recovered, but Grandfather died late that night. His pastor, Rev. J.H. Blair, arrived from Hamilton several hours later, but by then "O.B.," as he was known, was gone to be with his Lord.

Dick had known O.B. Griffin since he was a teenage preacher, and made the comment that, "Like Enoch, 'He walked with God, and God took him.'"

A Time to Keep Silent, and a Time to Speak
(Ecclesiastes 3:11)

Bert did not profess to be a born-again Christian. He was a good-hearted man and always willing to lend a hand. He came to church regularly with his wife and daughter who were members. Many times it was obvious that the Holy Spirit was convicting Bert of his need to yield to God, but he resisted God's call to repentance.

One night, after a rally in Cobourg, he was driving home to Oshawa. The car was full with him, his wife, Dick and Olive, and two other men. It was a bitterly cold night. The wind was whipping the snow about wildly, and drifts had formed across the pavement in many places. As he came around a curve in the road, he was confronted with a tractor-trailer taking more that its share of the road. With adroit steering, Bert avoided a head-on collision, but there was a serious side-swipe. The car was knocked off the road, over the shoulder, and into a fence, flipping almost over, but settling on all four wheels. No one was hurt, but the car was damaged sufficiently that it could not be driven.

Passing cars took the ladies on to Oshawa, and the two men also got rides. Dick remained with Bert. The truck driver promised to send a tow truck, and after what seemed like many hours, it finally came. In the meantime, since they could not sit in the overturned car, Dick and Bert walked, trying to keep warm. Back and forth, walking and waiting.

It seems like a very normal story up this point, and in fact, it was; something that happens every day. But one week later...

They had had very little conversation as they walked – for over two hours. Dick did not try to preach at Bert, since he knew the truth of Ecclesiastes 3. Blessed is the man who can discern just what "time" it is.

The following Sunday night Bert was in church as usual. When the altar call was given, Bert immediately stepped out and knelt at the altar to pray. When he had 'prayed through' and had the witness of the Holy Spirit that he was born again, he stood and gave this testimony:

"I have come to this church for years and have heard some great preaching, some by Pastor Bombay. I enjoy the singing here, but none of these things persuaded me to be a Christian.

"But last Monday evening I had a car accident on the way home from the rally in Cobourg. All the other passengers were sent home, but the pastor stayed with me. We walked for hours trying to keep warm. He never blamed anyone. He never preached at me. He just stayed with me. That's what I call real Christianity, and that's the kind of Christian I want to be. He prayed with me at the altar tonight, and I know that he and the Lord will help me in my Christian life."

With that, he went to Dick and put his arms around him as they wept tears of joy together. Bert never turned back. Does it make you think of Quartus in Romans 16:23? Just a brother!

16

Dick – The Man of Laughter

A merry heart does good, like medicine, but a broken spirit dries the bones (Proverbs 17:22).

Dick was a man with an unusually active sense of humour. He enjoyed a good laugh and would often manipulate the use of words to create a good laugh. No "dry bones" in his body! His vocabulary was seemingly endless, and the most often played games in our home were 'word' games.

The use of humour was in the home, in company, in the pulpit, and in committee meetings. Often, during a tense moment in a committee meeting when it seemed there was a deadlock, or feelings rather than reason were surfacing, he'd crack an off-the-cuff remark causing laughter, relaxation, and a renewed discussion with a lightened atmosphere.

His joking was always appropriate, both in content and to the situation. Quick-witted and applicable spontaneous remarks would open closed doors and closed minds.

Although he never said it in so many words, Dick seemed to feel that humour is an integral part of Christian ministry. Laughter has saved many a pending peril.

Don Macdonald was an example of a laugh saving the day, and probably a soul.

Don was a young Scotsman who came to Canada from Sterna to make his way in a new land as many had before him. In time, he fell among evil companions and began to follow in their ways, very much against his own upbringing and conscience.

Someone, somewhere, got to him with the Gospel, and he surrendered to the Lord. But he was in a quandary. He did not know where to go for fellowship.

One Sunday, Don was walking with a young lady from his place of employment, and he told her about some of his feelings and his dilemma. He wanted to follow the Lord, but did not know what to do. There was no church of his ancestry in Oshawa. Where should he go? It happened that, just at that moment, they were passing the old Evangel Tabernacle on King Street West, and, though she was not a Christian, she told him to go there. Perhaps they could tell him what he wanted to know; what he was looking for.

They parted company, and he never saw her again except at their place of employment.

Dick went down early from the apartment above the hall which served as the church. He saw this young man settled in a seat, usually reserved for the usher, in the back. Dick talked with Don for a while, then asked him if he would like to sit a little further forward. He did and felt he was comfortably in the right place. In that first meeting, when the invitation was given for people to simply come to the altar and spend some time in prayer, Don felt comfortable enough to do it. He continued to come to the services.

Several weeks later, Don received a powerful baptism in the Holy Ghost. For some time, he spoke in other tongues, and then prophesied. He also had a startling vision of the glory of the coming of Jesus Christ in the rapture. In fact, he was so impressed by his experience that he wanted Dick to go to the local newspaper and arrange for the whole front page of the newspaper to declare in big black bold letters, "JESUS IS COMING." Don said he would pay for it!

Dick told Don that he didn't think the newspaper would accept his proposed idea, but that indeed, the return of the Lord was imminent. Don described to Dick what he had seen in the vision, and it sounded something like what the Apostle John had written about in the Book of Revelation.

In the course of time, Don fell sick. Dick never heard what the precise diagnosis was, only that the doctor said he had a very short time to live. This so shocked Don that he turned again to "the bottle." Dick did not know this and did not see Don for some time. He finally tracked Don down through his cousin who reluctantly told Dick that Don had gone back to drinking, and drinking heavily. At that time, Don was in the hospital being treated for extreme alcoholism. They were trying to "dry him out."

Don was in a public ward. Dick stood for a moment in the doorway to see where Don was. Don saw Dick first and covered his face with both hands, peeking through his fingers like a child caught with his hand in the cookie jar. Dick stood silently at the foot of Don's bed until he finally took his hands away from his face. Then Dick burst out laughing!

Don said, "Go away, I'm not fit to talk to you!" He added a lot more to that. He said he was ashamed and asked why Dick had bothered to look him up. He continued to berate himself and said he was a terrible sinner.

That gave Dick an opening, and he told Don what he had told many an errant Christian. "His name is called Jesus, for He shall save His people from their sins." Dick prayed with him, and Don was reconciled to God. He never fell off the "water wagon" again.

It was many years later when Don told Dick, "If you had scolded me or berated me, I would not have listened. But when you stood there laughing, I knew you were not going to condemn me. I thought you would. It was your laughter that saved me!"

Don became a leader in the church and a helper of many people. He became a member of the church board. For a few years he even pastored a small church. He, like Job, knew the Lord through suffering, and he remained steadfast. All three of his daughters married ministers of the Gospel.

Dick often wondered about the Shepherd when he had found the lost sheep. Had he tears in his heart? More likely he had laughter and shouts of joy as he carried the wandering one back to the fold.

"Rejoice with me, for I have found my sheep which was lost!"

Balancing Humour With Rules

One day, Dick and his family were holidaying with his brother George's family in Souble Beach. Time came for family altar after the evening meal. A man in George's church was suffering from streptococcus, and before everyone took their turn in praying, this was mentioned as something that should be remembered in prayer. Each took their turn praying. Then it came time for George's son, Ken, to pray.

His prayer was, "God, please help the man with 'cockeye.'" Ken's brother, Doug, burst out with a snort and snicker.

Dick knew that his brother George was a very strict disciplinarian, and he got to George before George got to his son,

Doug, saying, "Take it easy, George. I could hardly keep from bursting out laughing myself!" Some things are funny, and you might just as well laugh!

The Chairman

On one occasion, while Dick was Assistant Superintendent, he had to chair the District Conference in Kingston while Rev. Wilbur Greenwood, the Superintendent, was sick. All conferences have their tensions, and Dick used humour to lighten these moments or just for a good time of humour. One of his favourite lines in response to any song leader asking people to stand to change their position was, "How can you possibly stand without changing your position?"

He had other lines he would throw out spontaneously. On one occasion, he called on the Women's Missionary Council to give their report. The report was given, including how many dollars had been raised for Missions and how many quilts had been sewn in the district as supplies for missionaries. Much of it centred around sewing for missionary children. When it was moved and seconded as a motion to accept the report, everyone raised their hands to vote its acceptance. With a grin, Dick said, "Well, I guess that sews that up!" In this very sedate setting, Mrs. Beulah Smith burst out laughing. She, too, was known for her sense of humour.

This particular conference called for unusual involvement of the Assistant Superintendent. Dick made the statement that, "Other than that conference, all I did was carry the Superintendent's briefcase a few times."

His joking was seldom the repetition of a structured joke. It was more spontaneous, off the cuff, sudden, and most often, totally unexpected. He was never irreverent, but he had little respect for "sacred cows." A wry remark with a straight face would often pass over the heads of many. He let it pass, rather than embarrass someone. He had scores of little funny poems which he would repeat, such as:

> "I eat my peas with honey,
> I've done so all my life,
> It makes the peas taste funny,
> But it keeps them on my knife."

Even when scolding one of his children, he'd end a very serious discussion with a remark like, "Thus endeth the first lesson!"

He enjoyed spoonerisms, and would often invent one on the spur of the moment, leaving people holding their sides and with tears in their eyes. As people laughed, he would sit quietly with a crooked grin on his face, looking pleased with himself. He enjoyed helping people enjoy life.

Yet, for all this, his head and heart were always on the lookout for opportunities to help, to answer questions, to minister comfort, to exhort, to love, and to heal. His very presence, whether in serious or hilarious circumstances, was calming.

17

Miracles Kept Happening

A Paraplegic Healed

When World War II finally came to an end, there were many young veterans looking for work. One of them was Clare Shank. Dick had married Clare and Edna when they were just eighteen.

Jobs were scarce, and two young veterans, members of Dick's church in Oshawa, decided to go into business for themselves. During the war, many homes remained unpainted, so Clare and Ernie went into the house-painting business.

It was a promising business, and things went well until a serious accident interrupted their progress. Clare was at the top of a ladder while Ernie held the base of the ladder firmly. No one understands how it happened, but suddenly Clare found himself falling. In the fall, his legs tangled in the ladder rungs, with his head and shoulders on the other side of the ladder. He stopped falling but in the process was seriously injured.

In the hospital, the doctors found that his back was broken, but that also several vertebrae were crushed. His left leg was completely paralyzed. During surgery, they took splinters from his shins and grafted them onto the crushed vertebrae. Eventually, the splinters fused with the crushed vertebrae, but this totally immobilized much of his spine. At that point, they learned that he would not have the use of his left leg – *ever.*

In the military hospital, they told Clare that he should accept the fact that he would never walk properly again, and that he should prepare himself under their guidance to be a cripple for the rest of his life. Clare was fit with a brace on his left leg from knee to toes, with another brace around his body, like a corset, to support his back. He was told that he would "always have to wear the braces and use a cane for the rest of his life."

The future looked gloomy, but his wife, parents, and the church made it a matter of continual prayer. For nine months he underwent therapy in different institutions, and Clare continued to hope in God.

One Sunday, in the prayer room of the Simcoe Street Pentecostal Church, he was sitting praying with his left leg stuck out in front of him. People had been praying for him. He wiggled his big toe. That was not supposed to be possible! There was rejoicing in the prayer room that night. Clare and Edna went home, planning to tell their doctor of these miraculous developments. Clare was amazed and excited. He actually saw his big toe wiggle!

Within a few days, Clare told his doctor that he was sure he had moved the big toe on his left foot. The doctor responded, "Impossible!" But when Clare was not looking, the doctor stuck a pin in Clare's big toe. Clare winced! But it was the decision of several doctors that it had only been his imagination. Yet it *was* true!

Finally, when his right leg had gained some strength, they graduated him to crutches. The other leg hung useless. They fit it with a mechanical device so that it would swing and drag as he got along on his crutches. Amazingly, he was eventually able to get along with just two canes, together with a metal body-frame to hold up his back. All the while, his church and family continued to pray for him.

Then, one unforgettable night at church, he was prayed for once again. Dick and the elders anointed him with oil according to scriptural instructions, laid hands on him, and prayed. As he sat down, he began to move the toes on his left foot. He stood to his feet again and began to walk without his canes. When he got home and took off his leg brace, he found he could still walk. Then, when he took off his body brace, he found he could stand erect, move normally, and walk without it. He never put it on again!

He was in church the next night and showed what he could do. He and his wife, Edna, along with their baby, rode home from church on the bus. As they alighted from the bus, without thinking, Clare picked up the baby and carried the baby from the bus stop to their home. Edna said that she was terrified when he did this, lest it be too much, but she refrained from saying anything. When they got indoors, she asked Clare, "Do you know what you have done?"

It was at that moment that they both realized Clare had been totally and completely healed.

However, that was not the end. Clare secured a job as a door-to-door salesman. It was winter, and the streets were icy. While walking between two houses, his feet went out from under him, and he fell – right on the spot where the splints had been fused to the crushed vertebrae. He lay on his back for some time, fearful of even trying to move. Finally, and cautiously, he rolled over, got to his hands and knees with no pain, then got to his feet. Just as cautiously, he bent his back and, to his surprise, realized he *could* bend it. Apparently, the fall had loosed the immobilized vertebrae!

As a veteran, he was required to return for periodic examinations, and when they X-rayed him, there was a new surprise. It was found that not only were the fused vertebrae separated, but the splints which had been implanted from his shins were completely gone – somewhere!

Clare has been a successful businessman and, along with his wife, served God faithfully in the Oshawa church for years. They have even spent time in missionary work overseas.

Dick went hunting with Clare on one occasion, and they travelled up and down hills, through rough country for four days on foot. Dick could not restrain a question, "Do your back or legs ever let you down?" Clare replied, "I never take any notice of them."

Nothing is too hard for God!

A Real Miracle Service

In those days, the Sunday evening service was an evangelistic outreach. The whole church was aware of the fact that in all probability, Dick, their pastor, would give an invitation from the pulpit for people to repent and be saved. This particular service was not out of character. Everything was proceeding as normal, and the sermon was meant to prepare the way for sinners to come to Christ for salvation.

Dick was often heard advising younger pastors to "preach for what you want to happen. If you want to see people saved, preach salvation from the Word. If you want to see people healed, preach healing from the Word. If you want to see people baptized in the Holy Spirit, preach it from the Word. Then expect it to happen, and clearly instruct people in their specific requests from the Lord."

However, in this case, as Dick began to preach, he found himself digressing and talking about the power of Christ to heal. Two or three times he returned to his prepared subject, "salvation," but each time found himself drifting in the same direction again.

He began to realize that God must have a purpose in it and was nudging him to do what He wanted. So, for a few minutes, Dick presented Jesus Christ as the Healer. The Holy Spirit came with great anointing on him, and the congregation was responding with a sense of expectancy and anticipation.

After concluding his revised sermon, he invited *anyone* who needed *anything* from God to come forward and to stand in front of the altar. Immediately, sixteen men and women stood to their feet from various parts of the congregation, came, and stood in a line across the front of the church. The elders of the church were then invited to stand behind these supplicants and to join in praying for them.

Dick began at one end of the line and asked the first man, "What do you want the Lord to do for you?" With a rather surprised look, the man answered, "Not a thing! As soon as I stood to my feet I felt God's power, and I am healed!" And it was a fact! Everyone knew this man was sick. He was on leave from General Motors with a serious heart condition. Dick told him to turn to the congregation and testify as to what God had done for him. He did, and there was great rejoicing. He returned to work at General Motors and worked right through until retirement. He died at a good old age, twenty-one years after retirement. Brother Teskey was well known in the church.

Dick moved on to the next person, this time a lady, and asked what she wanted the Lord to do for her. She looked a little bewildered as she replied, "The same thing happened to me as happened to Brother Teskey." She also testified, causing great and very audible rejoicing in the church.

Strange, you may think? Yes, wonderfully strange! Dick asked the same question of the next fourteen people, and all but two reported they had been healed as soon as they stood to their feet to come to the altar.

The two who did not report immediate healing came back later to report that they too had been healed saying they had not been able to test their healing immediately.

"The power of the Lord was present to heal..." (Luke 5:17). Also, as Psalm 107:20 says, "He sent His word and healed them, and delivered them from their destructions."

The Case of the Reluctant Husband

One of the great concerns for Pastor Bombay was the matter of husbands who remained unsaved. They simply would not make any kind of move toward God, and certainly not a public commitment to Jesus as Lord of their lives. Some would have nothing to do with their wives' "religion." Others simply dismissed it as unimportant. Some accompanied their wives to church, but never responded to any invitations to repent and be saved.

This was about to change – dramatically. So much so that Dick's brother George once made the comment, "Dick has more men in his church per capita than any other P.A.O.C. pastor I know of!" This was due to the fact that Dick began men's prayer meetings on a weekly basis, and the men interceded for specific men to be saved, delivered, and brought into fellowship with the church. Dick had a strong conviction that the father should be a priest in the home, offering spiritual leadership in both prayer and the process of family decision-making.

Over the years, God gave Dick a good deal of success in winning men to God and the church. A case in point was Ernie.

Never one to skirt an issue, Dick asked Ernie's wife, who was a faithful member of the church, to arrange a meeting for him and Ernie. The wife was afraid of Ernie's reaction. Apparently, Ernie didn't have much use for preachers, particularly Pentecostal preachers. He had often stated his annoyance that his wife attended a church "where they make so much noise." But she never stopped praying for him.

When Dick finally succeeded in visiting this reluctant husband one evening, he must have made some kind of impression, for Ernie told his wife that he "rather liked him." But that's as far as it went. Several years later, when Dick finally left Oshawa, Ernie was one of the few husbands who had not been saved and come into the church.

All the children were grown. Two daughters had married preachers, and a son had become a deacon and the treasurer of the church. Finally, Ernie's wife died, and he was left alone.

Dick was invited back to conduct a wedding in the church in Oshawa, and he was asked to be at the rehearsal on the previous Friday evening. Friends invited Dick and Olive to stay with them overnight and to go to the wedding with them.

The next morning, before the wedding, when Dick awakened, he began to think about Ernie whom he had not seen for several years. A growing urge to visit him occupied his mind, so he prayed that the Lord would help direct him and prepare Ernie's heart for the visit.

Ernie was just putting his golf clubs into the trunk of his car when Dick pulled into the driveway behind him. They shook hands, and Dick remarked that he would not want to keep him from his game. It was also quite apparent that Ernie wanted to get away, so Dick took the plunge and said, "Ernie, I have been very much concerned about you, particularly since your wife died. I felt strongly impressed to see you today and to talk to you about getting saved." He stared at Dick for a brief moment, then slammed down the lid of his trunk and said, "Come on inside!"

The last time he had been in a church was for his wife's funeral, even though he lived just a block from one of the branch churches in Oshawa.

They talked for a while, and when Dick asked him the direct question, "Ernie, do you want to be saved?" Ernie surprised Dick with his answer: "I don't know how. What should I do to be saved?"

Pastor Bombay soon enlightened him, inviting him to kneel and ask the Lord to save him. But they never got to their knees. Just at that inopportune moment, some visiting relatives arrived at the door. Dick remained only long enough to be introduced, and then left with a sense of disappointment.

Dick called the local pastor whom he knew, related what had happened, and asked him to visit Ernie as soon as possible.

But Ernie made the first move. God had really been at work.

Shortly after Dick arrived at his office in Belleville on the following Monday morning, he had a call from Pastor Fred Spring. He said, "I was surprised to see Ernie in church Sunday morning. When I finished preaching, I closed the meeting in prayer. When I opened my eyes, Ernie was kneeling at the altar. I asked the people to remain in prayer as I went down to the altar to pray with him. When he finally stood to his feet, he gave a beautiful testimony."

Following that urge of the Spirit of God caused Dick great joy, knowing that, had he not, Ernie may not have followed through by going to church that next Sunday morning.

Later, when Ernie Hughes retired, he went to live with a son in Windsor. Then he moved to Claresholm, Alberta, to live with a daughter, Mrs. Dick Cooper, whose husband was the pastor of the local Pentecostal church. Ernie became sick and was hospitalized at eighty-two years of age, twenty-six years after he accepted the Lord. Each time his daughter Glynis, and her husband, Pastor Dick Cooper, visited him in the hospital, he asked them to pray with him. When he died, his body was returned to Oshawa for burial.

Dick was asked to conduct the funeral, and, during his message entitled, "How to Become a Christian," he wove the story of

Ernie's conversion into it. All of the children and their spouses were present, and none of them had heard the story before.

There really can be joy at a funeral!

This sensitivity to the urges and leadings of the Holy Spirit characterized Dad's life. I can remember a time when we were having family altar after our evening meal. This was a normal practice in our home. The Scripture would be read, then we would kneel at our chairs around the table, and each of us would lead out in prayer. In this particular incident, I remember Dad getting off his knees, walking straight to the hall closet where we lived at 37 Fairbanks Street in Oshawa. Without explanation, he put on his hat and coat, went out the door, got into his old hand-painted blue Plymouth, and was gone. The Spirit of God had nudged him to visit someone. I don't remember just what that particular situation was about.

But Dad listened to that inner voice of the Spirit.

18

Holidays

Dad didn't always find it easy to get holidays. And when he did, it could very well be interrupted by a serious problem or the death of a church member. He would leave Mom and the rest of us, drive back to Oshawa to minister to the family, conduct the funeral, and then return. It didn't give him much of a holiday, but when he returned, he'd become relaxed, ready for fishing, swimming, whittling whistles, or making sling shots for David and me.

He loved the North country. It, to him, was the most relaxing and refreshing place in the world. He called it "God's country." He taught us all to love nature, and Northern Ontario especially. He seemed to know the name of every tree and bush God planted in Muskoka.

He always took us to High Falls, where he'd point out, with a little bit of pride, where his father, John, had built a bridge over the top, and which, reportedly, would take any load anyone cared to drive across. Even though it was made of what appeared to be only two-inch angle iron, it was cleverly constructed and braced. The wooden deck of the bridge had long gone, rotted away by years of use and then weather. Now, the whole thing is gone. But it shortened the journey for many a family travelling to Bracebridge.

We spent our holidays in the cottage Dad built at the foot of the hill behind the old frame house on Woodward Street in Bracebridge. It seemed to be cut off from the whole world. Across the river was "Flat Rock," a fairly smooth slanting rock which provided a great run-and-leap into the Muskoka River. Many a memory from his youth would come out as we sat on that great sweep of granite.

The cottage was surrounded by tall, stately pines and birch trees, the bush cleared from around the cottage. We usually approached it from across the river, where Dad would park the car. Dad had built a homemade punt out of plywood, and this was our transport across the river to the cottage. It was also our fishing boat, where I learned to love fishing as a sport, as well as a source of fresh, ready-to-fry bass.

Dad would usually squeeze out two weeks of the summer for the family to go north to Bracebridge. He loved the north woods and that old 'home' location on the Muskoka River. Walks through the town of Bracebridge were filled with his memories of people, places, and incidents from his youth.

One of those stories stands out in my memory. Dad had been sent to the store to get some mothballs by his mother, Nettie. As he came out of the store, he was hailed by a fellow in town who was just a few bricks short of a full load. This fellow was always pestering everyone to share any candy they might have as they came out of the store. He was a harmless fellow but, to Dick, sometimes annoying. His greeting to Dick, as usual, was, "Giz's a candy, Dick, giz's a candy." The paper bag looked like candy. Dad said, "I don't have any." The fellow said, "Ah, c'mon, Dick, giz's a candy."

Now Dad was not always the almost-perfect person that many have assumed. The old Nick rose up in Dad, and he grinned as he told us what he did. He reached into the bag, pulled out a moth ball, and handed it to the fellow. In a flash, the mothball was in the fellow's mouth, and in seconds, it was back out with the exclamation, "Ahh, Dick!"

On those holidays, Dad would often take us out to where the old log farmhouse had stood. We were shown the sunken place where it had been, where the cow and horse shed had been, and where the chickens had stumbled around drunk. We visited the graveyard where Dad pointed out the graves of former friends, and the rock on which Ed, his brother, had seen their long dead sister, Bertha. He pointed out trees he had planted, and where he'd picked blueberries. He delighted in sharing information about his joy as a boy. From the way he told it, you'd never know about the abject poverty in which he was raised.

Those holidays were like medicine, real good medicine for Dad – for all of us. Swimming, fishing, and following the same paths which Dad had run in his bare feet were a delight. We had to walk tenderly on those paths though; we were used to shoes year 'round.

Often, we could see Dad sitting on the dock in front of the cottage. The look on his face alone was enough to make us happy too. He sat there, remembering and breathing the sweet air of his beloved north country. He taught us all to appreciate the woods, rivers, and clear skies of Muskoka. Every chance I have, I pass by that old property where a new house has long since replaced the old tumble town frame house. Some of the massive pines still stand there.

I go out to the old farm and wonder how they ever lived there. I pick a wild flower and keep it in my car until it wilts. I look at the property and resent the tall radio tower put there by the trucking company which hauls gravel out of that area. Sometimes you wish the past could come back for a while....

Dad would often go by the farm on his travels to the churches as he fulfilled his duties as District Superintendent. When he retired (as much as he could), he would occasionally head north, just to be near his past.

On one occasion, I was given a free 'round-trip ticket on an inaugural flight from Nairobi to New York. I paid the extra fare and spent a week with Dad driving through Muskoka and visiting friends.

A Hat Full of Blueberries

Dick was raised in Muskoka. It is possibly the most naturally beautiful, wild, yet orderly piece of God's real estate to be found anywhere. The family home in Bracebridge backed onto the Muskoka River. A very high, tree-covered hill led from the river up to the old homestead. (In 1952, he bought the old property from his sister Dorothy.)

Dad wrote once,

"I re-furbished the old house, and I remember, after a hard day's work, telling my son Calvin of many of the incidents which took place in that old house. Wood frame, and somewhat run down, it was home for years.

"One day, while I was out alone, remembering my youth, I parked beside a country road and wandered over some rocks, and behold: a patch of blueberries! They were big and luscious and wild. I had no container in the car, so I filled my floppy cap and carried it carefully to the car. I drove along the road until I saw what appeared to be a dairy farm; the pasture was filled with healthy looking black and white Holsteins. An idea began to form.

"My thoughts went back to my boyhood when we lived on the farm. When we had blueberries, we smothered them with thick cream, and doused them with brown sugar. Wouldn't that taste good again!!?

"The idea had fully formed.

"I turned into the lane that led to the house and drove around back. There sat a white-haired lady on the stoop. She looked rather startled, but the dog came to me wagging his tail, and I followed him from the car. I assured the lady I would do her no harm, and she smiled and asked what she could do for me.

"I told her about finding the blueberries and that it had made me think of my boyhood and the cream and the sugar. I wondered if she had any real thick cream, and could I have a bowl and some sugar right there? She replied that she certainly did have such cream and would get me what I asked. I told her I would be glad to pay whatever she asked.

"She invited me to sit on the steps while she went inside. Soon she returned with a bowl, a jug, a sugar bowl, and a spoon. 'Help yourself,' she said. I did! It was the kind of cream that went PHLOP, PHLOP when I poured it. I enjoyed that hat full of berries!

"We chatted while I slowly ate those berries, remembering days long gone. I didn't know who she was, and she never asked who I was. We just sat and talked as though we were old friends. When I was about to leave, I asked, 'How much do I owe you for all this?' I was delighted by her answer. 'I have enjoyed so much watching you enjoy those berries and cream like when you were a boy, that you don't owe me a thing.' I insisted, but she refused.

"It was one of those care-free and happy interludes in life that I will remember as long as I live. I could not find that farm again if I tried, but I will never forget the white-haired lady with the twinkle in her eyes who lived there."

When Dad became District Superintendent of Eastern Ontario and Quebec District of the Pentecostal Assemblies of Canada, he had to move to Belleville. He sold that cottage on the

Muskoka River, but the yearning for the North never left him – or any of us, for that matter.

Belleville was a city on the Bay of Quinte, but for some reason, the waters there could not compare to the waters of a northern lake. Dad bought another property and built another cottage on Cashel Lake, many miles north of Belleville. Two sons by then were married, and Ruth was about to be married. These times away enriched their romances when they visited that cottage with Mom and Dad.

Lois and Rick probably got as much mileage as anyone from that peaceful, secluded place with loons calling throughout the day. Again, Dad found a haven for retreat and refreshment, sometimes with just Mom.

That was also where Dad taught Rick how to tip a canoe, and he's been doing that on people ever since.

19

Twenty Odd Years in Oshawa

Dick never wanted to be the pastor of a monster church. He said there was always a place for them in major cities, especially as an evangelistic centre. His vision was for many churches throughout a city and in nearby towns. He would often "lift up his eyes, and look on the fields which were ready for harvest." I think he felt that the more harvesters there were, the greater the harvest. He certainly proved that true in Oshawa.

Back when the Canadian Census still had the question, "To what denomination do you belong?" Oshawa, of all the cities in Canada, showed the highest percentage of Pentecostal members and adherents.

It was largely due to his "divide and multiply" principle. When the church on Simcoe Street South got filled up to the last row, he would put his tactic into motion. If members of the board lived in an area where there was no Pentecostal church, he'd ask if they'd be willing to help in the leadership and founding of another church. They usually were willing. Then he'd ask the congregation who lived in that same area if they would be willing to start attending the new church.

Either Dad's assistant pastor would be transferred to become the pastor, or a person would be brought in. The Simcoe Street church would financially sponsor the new church until it was self-supporting. If my memory serves me right, Dad was involved in starting at least three new churches in Oshawa, and another three in neighbouring towns.

My cousin, now the Rev. Ken Bombay, overheard Dad telling Mom what had happened when he came in late one evening. Dad had a meeting for people in nearby Whitby. There were seventeen people present. At the end of the prayer and Bible study period, Dad asked the group how many would be interested in starting regular meetings in Whitby. Twelve responded positively. Dad said to Mom, "I think we should start a work in Whitby." And he didn't just think about it!

I recall my own involvement as a kid of about eight, going to the town hall in Whitby with Dad where the first regular meetings were held on Sunday afternoons. There was a five-inch steel post in the middle of the hall, and I'd take my position by that post, handing out hymn books to the folks who came. Dad would lead the singing, ask one of the members of the Oshawa church who lived in Whitby to pray and take up the offering. Then he would do the preaching. He involved as many people as possible in his church planting efforts. Efforts, by the way, which never once failed.

That meeting in the Whitby Town Hall eventually grew into a self-supporting congregation which built one church, outgrew it, and built again.

One of the churches Dad helped establish was what is now the King Street Pentecostal Church, in the western part of Oshawa.

It began thus:

It was the Christmas season, and a group of children were carolling in the College Hill area of Oshawa. They came to the door of one of the members of Dick's church, and when they began to sing, Frank Danzey invited them in. As he was handing out candies to them, he asked them where they had learned the carols. "At school," they said. Thinking they were talking about a Sunday School, Frank asked them which one. They replied that they didn't go to a Sunday School but had learned them at public school.

"How would you like to come back on Sunday afternoon, and we'll all sing some more carols?" Frank asked. So, apparently, with the parents' consent, they had a house full.

Frank was a music teacher, and both he and his wife had taught Sunday School for English speaking Slavic children in the Slavic Pentecostal Church. With the music as the centre, and very spontaneously entered into, their Sunday "sing" became a big thing in the neighbourhood. It grew each week until the house was full of children and they found it impossible to manage alone. That was when they called Dick and told him of their "problem."

"I would like to start a regular Sunday School, but I have no teachers for classes. Can you help?"

Words of that nature to Dick Bombay were like saying "Sic 'em" to a dog.

At the next youth meeting in his church, Dick explained the situation and asked for volunteers. Eight young people volunteered, including the youth leader and his wife. They were organized into a Sunday School staff and were sent to Frank Danzey's house the very next Sunday. Every room in the house was used as a classroom, including the basement.

Frank Danzey's son was in Bible College at the time, and as soon as he graduated, he came home and took charge. He was a mechanical technician, so was able to support himself while he gave all his spare time to the growing group of Sunday School pupils. The "mother" church on Simcoe Street supplied all the teaching materials and the youth, who were already involved in their own Sunday School. But they continued to help in the Danzey home every Sunday afternoon.

Earl Danzey, Frank's son, soon found out that there were adults who wanted to attend the Sunday School as well, and thus began an adult class. Soon after, a Sunday morning service was begun, and then a mid-week prayer and Bible Study.

The story reminds one of the camel that stuck its head in the tent and eventually took over the whole tent. Something had to be done. They began to talk about building a church. Since Dick was the local Presbyter of the Pentecostal Assemblies of Canada, he was invited to join in the discussions, especially when it came to the matter of financing the project.

The "mother" church helped financially, but Dick did an almost unheard-of thing. On the day of the dedication of the church, he encouraged thirty-seven members of his own church to transfer their membership to the new College Hill Church. He concentrated on those especially who lived closest to the new church. Over the next few years, a few more members joined them, providing the new church with experienced and godly board members who had already served on the board of the "mother" church. That church thrived, built a new church building, outgrew it, then built finally on King Street West where growth is still the norm.

When you are building the right Kingdom, competition becomes unknown, and church growth becomes natural, supernaturally!

Let's Start Another

In the northern part of the city of Oshawa, there was no evangelical church and witness. The growth of the city was rapidly moving north, and more and more homes and businesses were moving into the area. The mother church felt a distant but distinct birth pang. The possibility of sponsoring a church in that area moved from possibility to planning, and to the first steps. Finding a location could take time, so a plan was devised to park a Sunday School bus on a supermarket parking lot. The shopping center agreed and installed an electric outlet on a pole so the bus could have light and heat.

Some of the people who had volunteered to help at College Hill were now free, and they were asked if they would be willing to man the bus and lead the Sunday School. I was, by then, sixteen years of age and, wanting to help, became one of the drivers/teachers on this new venture. Ed and Dot Wright gave splendid overall leadership to this new venture.

It soon became evident that a building was needed, and the need was getting urgent. The Simcoe Street Church board found a property within easy walking distance from the "Parked Bus Church," and purchased it. It consisted of a block of eight building lots. It was decided to build what became known as a "parsonage church." In other words, the parsonage would be built first, without some of its inner walls, and used as a Sunday School and church until they could expand no further. When church and Sunday School outgrew it, then the church was to be built on the adjoining lots. Then the inner walls would be built in the original building and converted into a parsonage.

By this time, Dick had another assistant pastor, who was placed in charge of the Sunday School, although he continued to help Dick in both visitation and preaching at the mother church on Simcoe Street.

It was at this time that Dick and Olive were approached by the Foreign Missions department of the Pentecostal Assemblies of Canada and asked if they would take a leave of absence from the church in Oshawa (where they had been for twenty-two years already) to go to Nairobi, Kenya, and build an International Center. After much thought and prayer, they felt it was the right thing to do.

The interim pastor took little interest in the north end of the city, and Dick's assistant was called to another church in another city. A new assistant pastor came in, and he was given charge of what was happening in the north end of Oshawa. The new assistant pastor began regular services, as well as continued the Sunday School in the parsonage church. By the time Dick returned from Africa, two years later, the assistant was devoting his full time to the new Byng Avenue Church.

But some problems had arisen. With no encouragement from the interim pastor of the mother church, discouragement had begun to grip some of those involved. There was talk of closing it down and writing it off as a "learning experience." Ed Wright couldn't see it that way at all, and he pressed for there to be a delay until Dick got back from Africa. He said, "Brother Bombay is coming home shortly, so let's wait until then and see what he says."

They waited.

When Dick got back, he was quickly acquainted with all the details, and together with men of faith, they decided to move ahead and build a church. Once again, the mother church on Simcoe Street assumed the financial responsibility of the building and paid the pastor's salary.

Then one day, in a joint meeting of both church boards, it was decided that the new church and board would take on the responsibility for the mortgage. The mother church gave them a substantial financial gift to speed them on their way, as well as an invitation to "give us a shout" if they ever got into financial difficulty. They never did!

Since then the church has been enlarged, and additional facilities added. There is now a Pentecostal church in every quarter of the city of Oshawa, a city which just keeps on growing.

There was a tradition that began in the Simcoe Street Pentecostal Church over the years. On Christmas Day, a great homecoming would take place.

Dozens of young people had grown up in that church. Dick consistently involved young and old alike in the ministry of the church. It was never a one-man show, or a one-family affair. Dick kept our exposure as his children to a minimum, although he never left us out. He would recognize young men and women with gifts and abilities and put them to work.

Many felt gifted and called to the ministry, and were trained, both in the local church and at the Eastern Pentecostal Bible College. Literally scores of young people had their ministry beginnings in that congregation. Back in about 1960, someone took it upon themselves to list the people who were pastors, evangelists, and missionaries who came out of that church. At that tim, it totaled at least forty to fifty, and the trend continued. Many more have since gone from that church into ministry.

It had become customary at Christmas time for any of these preachers and their wives who could to descend on Oshawa to be with their parents for Christmas and to enjoy a great Christmas Day church service. It was a highlight of the year in that church.

What Are Hands For?

Jim was one of those young preachers who came home one Christmas and asked if he could see Pastor Bombay. He sat down opposite Dick's desk in the office and, without much preamble, told how very discouraged he was. There was no progress in his little church far up north. Crowds were not crowds. There was just a sprinkling of members whose interest in the things of God seemed rather weak. And loneliness was not the least of his problems.

Jim had come up through the Sunday School, felt the call of God, graduated from Bible College, and been licensed to preach.

Dick had prayed with him when he had been saved and become a Christian. He had also prayed with Jim when he had been filled with the Holy Spirit and spoke in other tongues. He was a great young fellow, but now he was ready to quit.

In his agitation, Jim stood and paced the office while he poured out his discouragement to Dick. He was leaning with his hands on the desk, facing Dick, when suddenly Dick asked him, "Jim, what are those things on the ends of your arms?" Jim looked bewildered as he returned, hesitantly, "Do you mean my hands?" "Yes," Dick said. "What are you supposed to do with them?" Jim, now thoroughly confused, said, "I don't know what you mean!"

Dick picked up his Bible, which was always within reach, and opened it to Mark 16:18, "...they will lay hands on the sick, and they will recover."

Silence for a moment.

"Do you ever do that, Jim?" Dick asked. Jim could not remember that he ever had. The conversation continued for a while, then Dick and Jim prayed together. He left the office and went back to his little flock up north.

The following Easter, he was home in Oshawa again for a few days. Again he sat with Pastor Bombay in his office. He was different. There seemed to be an excitement about him, and finally, the story came out. This is the substance of what he told Dick:

"When I returned north, the first Sunday morning a woman requested prayer for her daughter. A serious condition had developed in the pre-natal period, and the doctor had said the complications would claim either the life of the mother or of the child; perhaps even both.

"As soon as the service was over, I went to their home in the country. The sick woman's mother and I prayed, and I remembered what you had told me. So both the mother and I laid hands on the daughter and prayed for her in the Name of the Lord as best I knew how.

"No change took place that I could see, and she seemed to be at death's door. I had to leave to prepare for the evening service.

"The next day, Monday, was an area rally day, and on this occasion they met in my church. The leaders of the meeting sat on the little platform, and I sat on the front pew. One of the leaders decided to call for testimonies, and the first was a voice from behind me. A young lady was telling how just yesterday she was so low, but the pastor came and prayed for her, and this morning she was feeling well and strong.

"Then, to my embarrassment, she said, 'There is my pastor in the front pew.' I turned to see for sure who it was, and there was the young lady we had prayed for just the day before."

It was a small community and everyone knew about her condition. As a result, her healing caused quite a stir in the whole area. New interest came in the church. It filled up with people.

Jim went on to say, "People listen to what I have to say." This seemed to surprise him.

In due time, the young lady delivered a fine healthy boy and both were well. The young mother gives all the glory to God, and since then, many others have been healed, and God is at work in that community.

Only One Last Chance!

While pastoring in Oshawa, Dick received a phone call from one of the church deacons. He had taken his little daughter in for a simple tonsillectomy. As he was leaving the hospital after a visit, the deacon had met an acquaintance who told him about her stepson.

Just outside the city, the stepson had been in a car paint shop when an explosion took place. He was terribly burned and was now in the emergency room. As a girl, this acquaintance had attended the church, and she asked if the deacon and Dick could come. Dick was in the middle of supper when the call came, but he dropped everything and went to the hospital.

Kenny, the boy who had been burned, had never been in the church or Sunday School. There had been a family break-up, then divorce, and a second marriage. No one seemed very concerned about the spiritual welfare of Kenny.

Dick was unable to see him on that first visit, since his life hung by a thread in intensive care. Dick and the deacon did have prayer with the stepmother and the father of the boy whom he had not met before that day. They were distraught. The explosion and fire that followed had destroyed the shop, as well as their home where they lived above the shop. Now it appeared they were going to lose the boy as well. Their anguish was palpable.

Young Kenny hung between life and death for about a week, during which time they transferred him to the Toronto General Hospital Burn Ward because of the intensity of his burns. Occasionally, he would show some signs of life, but most of the time he was in a coma.

Kenny's father called Dick and asked if he could come to Toronto immediately. The doctors had phoned to tell them that Kenny was dying and there was nothing else they could do. Special permission was needed to enter the room. Permission was given, but when they arrived, the head nurse said there was little use in going in, since Kenny had been "out" for several days, showing no responses whatsoever. But both the father and Dick insisted they go in. They were restricted to entering the room one at a time.

Dick was asked by the father to go in first. He was fitted with gown, mask, and gloves. As he walked over to the bed, Dick said, "Kenny?" To Dick's surprise, Kenny's eyes had opened, just a slit. All his face and upper body were swollen and disfigured beyond description or recognition.

Dick then asked him, "Kenny, do you know who I am?" Kenny's head nodded perceptibly. Quickly and plainly, Dick told

Kenny the "old, old story of Jesus and His love." Then he asked Kenny if he would believe that Jesus would receive him. Again, Kenny's head nodded a clear affirmative "yes." Dick told Kenny that he was going to pray for him and that he should repeat the words in his mind, even though he could not speak them. Dick watched as he prayed and was moved to see Kenny trying to form the words with his misshapen lips.

When he finished praying, he asked Kenny if he believed God had heard them. This time there was a more vigourous effort as he nodded "yes." Another question: Dick asked, "Do you feel peace in your heart?" This was answered by a last affirmative inclination of Kenny's head.

As Dick went out to where the father was waiting to see Kenny, he told the nurse what had happened. The nurse was incredulous. She quickly prepared the father to go in with gown, mask, and gloves. She went in with the father.

When they came out, just a short time later, the nurse turned to Dick and asked, "Are you certain his eyes opened, his lips moved, and he nodded his head?" Dick assured her that it was so. She said, "It must have been a miracle!" for when they went in, there was no response to his father's voice, nor did he show any sign of hearing.

Kenny died that night. He had only one chance, and he grasped it. "Whosoever shall call on the name of the Lord shall be saved." It's never too late!

Life Blood

Time of day had little to do with the working hours of a true pastor. And, as life would have it, some of the more memorable incidents took place in the dark of night.

Dick's desk sat by the front door of their modest manse. No big office for this pastor; no room!

One night, as Dick sat as his desk at about 11:00 p.m., a rapid knock came at the door. He reached over and opened the door immediately, and one of his deacons stepped in quickly. He seemed out of breath, but burst out with, "Edna, my daughter-in-law, is in the hospital, and she...." He was almost babbling. "She is bleeding uncontrollably. She must have her type of blood, and I have been trying all day to find someone with the right type. Now she is unconscious from loss of blood, and unless we find a donor she will die."

This was, of course, before the Oshawa hospital had its own plasma bank.

Allan Shank stuttered on, "Do you know anyone who has Type A 1?" Dick did not answer but reached into his desk and brought out his blood donors record. H showed it to the distraught father-in-law, saying, "Is this what you need?" The card showed, "Type A 1."

Allan was so surprised and relieved, he burst into tears, and then burst out, all in one breath, "Will you do it? How soon can you be ready?"

Dick replied, "I'm ready right now!" And off they went.

When they got to the hospital, Edna's condition had worsened, and there was no time for anything but a direct transfusion. Dick was wheeled into the room where she lay. From the look of her, she didn't look like she could last much longer. She was pitifully white and seemed to be shrunken. Her breathing was shallow and fitful.

Quickly, the necessary paraphernalia was attached to both Edna's and Dick's arms, and Dick watched as his blood flowed from his arm into hers. Staff stood tensely by, and in a remarkably short time, colour began to appear in her cheeks. Her breathing became stronger, and as the blood continued to slowly flow into her, her eyelids began to flutter and her breathing became more regular. Her eyes fluttered open, then closed again, then seemed to snap open. Her gaze was fixed on the ceiling for a moment, and a questioning look appeared on her face. It seemed to say quite plainly, "Where am I, and what's going on?"

Slowly, her eyes turned to Pastor Bombay, and she asked, "Brother Bombay, what are you doing here?" Dick was unable to answer, because he had suddenly become choked up with emotion. The doctor stepped into the silence of the unanswered question and breathed quietly, "You are all right, just lie quietly." After a while, Dick was wheeled out and given the usual coffee and a sweet biscuit.

Later, after the dizziness which often follows the giving of blood passed, Dick asked if he could see Edna. They allowed him in long enough to have prayer with her.

The next evening, Clare, her husband, phoned to tell the pastor that Edna would be coming home the next day. Life went on normally for Clare and Edna Shank. They have raised a fine Christian family.

There seems to be some parallel between this incident and the Scripture which says, "It is the blood that makes atonement for the soul." Dick has seen countless times what happens when a repentant sinner puts his faith in the life-giving blood of our Lord and Saviour, Jesus Christ.

20

War and Wisdom

When the Burden Rolled Away

The life of a soldier is not conducive to living a "nice" life, and, even though as a boy he had known the Lord, when he came back from World War II, this veteran lived a life a sin. He came to Ontario looking for a job, found one in Oshawa, and began appearing in the church from time to time. He made his way back to the Lord, but the real battle was still ahead.

He became a member of the church and attended faithfully. At the end of the evening services, he would respond to the place of prayer. After some time, Dick noticed that he lingered in the prayer room after others had left. He seemed to be in some distress and spent much time in prayer and in tears. Dick began to realize that the fellow had some serious problem.

Finally, one night, Dick knelt beside him and asked, "Is there any way I can help you?" The young man looked at Dick with swollen eyes and replied that he did not know if he could help or not. Dick told the man he could tell him as much or as little as he chose, but whatever he said would be held in confidence. He decided to tell all.

He poured out a tale of temptation and sin the likes of which Dick had heard many times before from others. When he concluded, he looked down and said, "Now I suppose you will kick me right out of the church." Dick replied, "Of course not. The Bible says, 'His Name shall be called Jesus, for He shall save *His people* from their sins.' This is what the church is here for, and you need the church."

Dick prayed for him, and he left, still looking rather disconsolate. He did not appear to evidence any change within or without.

Many months later, as Dick was greeting folks at the close of the service, the young man came by. Dick shook his hand and asked, "How are you?" He replied, "Fine!" Dick held on to his hand, and asked again, "How *are* you?"

With that, he held on to Dick's hand and drew him apart from the passing crowd leaving the church. He asked, "Do you remember *that* Sunday night in the prayer room?" Dick remembered, and said so. "Well, that night I went home and slept like a baby. Those things have never come back. I'm free, and have been ever since that night!"

A few years later, he became a deacon, and he has served God for many years. It makes you wonder if many more chains would be broken if only we took literally what James wrote:

> *Confess your trespasses to one another, and pray for one another, that you may be healed* (James 5:16).

The Baby-Sitter Problem

A young lady began attending church with her mother-in-law who was a deeply devoted Christian. In a few weeks, the young woman was saved, quite literally "born again," and began to attend almost every meeting. Her husband drove her to church but would not go in. Each Sunday morning, he would pick up his wife, mother, and daughter, and they would all go to the mother's house for dinner. Sunday night he would often bring his wife to church, and then return home to baby-sit the little girl by himself.

As the young mother's love for the Lord grew, so did her desire to be with God's people. She began coming to the women's meetings on Tuesday, the prayer meeting on Wednesday, and she brought her little daughter to the ladies prayer meeting on Thursday afternoon.

A few months went by, and the two ladies, mother and daughter-in-law, asked if they could talk to Pastor Bombay. There was a problem. Gordon, the young husband, objected to his wife leaving him at home to baby-sit their little girl on Sunday, Tuesday, and Wednesday evenings every week. It restricted his activity too much. He had no objection to bringing them to Sunday School and church in the morning, nor to the prayer meeting on Thursday afternoon.

The young man's mother was indignant with her son and did not hesitate to voice it. "I told Alice that if Gordon wanted to stay home and would not come with his wife to serve the Lord, then she should come anyhow and let him go to hell if he wanted to!"

Dick was shocked at this mother's apparently hard attitude, and he asked her how she squared that with what the Bible taught, "Wives, obey your husbands." Further conversation revealed that Gordon bowled each Tuesday evening, so Dick made a suggestion: "See if Gordon will agree to baby-sit on Wednesday evening, and you stay home on Tuesday and Sunday evenings. You will have Sunday School and the morning service on Sundays, Wednesday evening for prayer meetings, and the ladies prayer meeting on Thursday afternoons."

The mother-in-law made a quick switch and agreed fully. She urged Alice to try this... for a while.

A few weeks later, Gordon appeared in Sunday School and at the morning service with his wife and little girl. Soon they were all attending the Sunday evening service as well. It wasn't very long until Gordon was saved and a part of the Kingdom of God – and the problem was solved.

Both Gordon and Alice followed the Lord's instructions to be baptized, and both were filled with the Spirit, and in time, became members of the church.

Could this possibly be a practical exposition of what Peter wrote in 1 Peter 3:1-4?

> *Wives, likewise, be submissive to your own husbands, that even if some do not obey the word, they, without a word, may be won by the conduct of their wives, when they observe your chaste conduct accompanied by fear. Do not let your adornment be merely outward – arranging the hair, wearing gold, or putting on fine apparel – rather let it be the hidden person of the heart, with the incorruptible beauty of a gentle and quiet spirit, which is very precious in the sight of God.*

Dick's understanding and application of the Scriptures to the practical problems and situations in life earned him a reputation as a man of God, with a great deal of wisdom.

How to Destroy Faith

A great many children have been eternally destroyed because parents carelessly speak of the ministry, and fellow-Christians, in their presence. Even though they may be believing Christians, somewhere, sometime, they will have to answer for it.

Being a deacon in the church is no immunity against such terrible folly. One particular deacon, the father of several children, three of them still at home, was just such an example. He died while still a deacon in the church, leaving his wife with one son and two younger daughters. The son had not married and lived at home. That is where Dick met him. The young man was filling the gap, acting as a father to his two sisters.

Dick remarked that he had not seen him in church, and the young man evaded any invitation to come. This went on for several years. The only time he finally came was for the wedding of one of his younger sisters.

He was always pleasant with Pastor Bombay, even though Dick urged him time after time to come to the Lord and also to church. One day as the pastor was talking with him alone, the man said, "Pastor Bombay, I like you personally, but I am going to tell you why I don't go to your church." This is his story:

"We were brought up in your church before you ever came to Oshawa. My father was a deacon and my mother was a Sunday School teacher. Every Sunday we were there. I liked Pastor Ball. I liked his preaching.

"We had no car, so we walked to and from church together. On the way home, my parents would pull apart the sermon and say mean things about Mr. Ball. They criticized the people who testified in the meetings. I never heard them say anything good about the church. I don't even know why they continued going to the church!

"This same kind of talk would go on while we ate our dinner. It was this way every Sunday. I came to believe that the preacher and all the people were hypocrites – that they must be one thing in church, and another thing at home, just like my parents. I have lost all confidence in the church and the people, and I have no desire at all to go to church."

The only time that young man was ever seen in church was at a wedding, or at the funeral of his own mother, and then he came only as a gesture of respect for the pastor who officiated at the funeral.

It would be a good idea to give some serious thought to the words of Jesus found in Luke 17:1-2:

> *Then He said to the disciples, "It is impossible that no offenses should come, but woe to him through whom they do come! It would be better for him if a millstone were hung around his neck, and he were thrown into the sea, than that he should offend one of these little ones."*

The Fruit of Submission

She was an independent and very determined young lady. She was a working girl and continued to work after she was married, which was not as common a practice then as it is today.

While Dick was on a short hunting trip with her husband, he was told about some of the manipulating she did to get her own way. The husband was not too pleased, but didn't know what do. Of course, she had no idea that her husband had talked to her pastor.

One day, many months later, with tears of frustration, she told Dick of her inability to persuade her husband to tithe. Knowing some of the tension that existed between the couple, Dick felt this could be an opportunity to "kill two birds with one stone," i.e. help her in the matter of Christian submission, and at the same time, help him to obey God in tithing.

Dick began to make a suggestion, "Since your husband is the one who earns the money...." She quickly interrupted and told him that she earned nearly as much as her husband, and that she was going to tithe *her* money, regardless!

Dick talked to her about submission, in its biblical context. He pointed out that since they were "two being one flesh," all they had was *theirs* not just his or hers. Perhaps that was the real root of this problem, although there were other tensions which existed in their relationship. She seemed to listen.

Dick urged her to pray for grace to be submissive to her husband. Also, at some future time, when the storm within her had become still, and at a convenient moment, she should remind her husband that he was the head of the home. She could then let him know, quietly and reasonably, how she felt about tithing their income, then leave it up to him to decide what they should do about it.

This took some time, since it was not an easy matter for her to become settled and quiet inside. She had a little history to overcome. But Dick felt confident that if she could bring herself to simply and honestly submit to her husband's judgement in matters, quite a few other problems would work out well, too. And they did.

Much later, she happily told Dick what God had done, first in her, and then how easy it was for them to agree about tithing. Dick really didn't have to ask what had happened, since it was quite obvious that a change had taken place in their relationship. After fourteen years of marriage, they began to act like newlyweds – publicly!

He had been a Christian, for she had insisted she would not marry him unless he was. So he asked Jesus to be his Saviour. But now he began to serve and seek Jesus as Lord in earnest. He was soon filled with the Holy Spirit. He became active, with her, in the church. Having a very good voice, he joined the choir and continued to serve God.

Neither of them ever knew that the other had talked to Pastor Bombay. Listening to marriage problems, or any problems for that matter, should be kept inviolate by the confidant, pastor, or otherwise. Perhaps the advice Jesus gave about prayer might equally apply here: "When you enter the closet shut the door... and when you come out, shut your mouth firmly" (Dick's Version).

Dick had an amazing way of applying biblical principles to every day problems. The Bible does have the answers.

He was frequently asked by Christian wives what they should do about tithing when their husbands were not saved and perhaps didn't even go to church. He never encouraged them to act independently in this matter.

One woman said to him, "My husband would kill me if he knew I was bringing a tithe of his wages to the church. He lets me handle all the money, and all he asks is enough to buy tobacco and pocket money. He doesn't even ask about the rest!"

Dick rather doubted that he would kill her, but the husband *had* sent her to church with swollen eyes. Once he burned her shoes and another time tore her umbrella to shreds to prevent her coming. But this was not because she tithed, for he hadn't found that out.

So, in brief, this is what Dick told her: "At some convenient time, when he is in a good mood, bring up the subject. Explain that this is what God requires of everybody, and ask him what he thinks about it. In the meantime, pray and trust God to help you select the right time and give you the right words and attitude."

Shortly after this, with a beaming face she told Dick, "I was scared to ask him, but I did! All he said was, 'Well, if that is what God and the church expects, OK. But I'll take half to my church and you take half to yours.'" So, that is what they did.

But that is not the end of the incident! A few weeks later, the man said to his wife, "I've been watching what others put in the plate, even businessmen. They drop in a quarter. So you take the tithe to your church, and I'll drop in a quarter as the rest of them do."

Though he sometimes still abused her, he never questioned her about the tithe, and she was free to attend her church.

Dick never looked at the church books to see who was or was not supporting the church. He felt he could preach and teach without bias if he left those details in the hands of the official treasurer of the church.

Out of the Pit

From the pulpit it is difficult to even guess at the problems faced by those who attend a church. One such mystery was a quiet, white-haired man who had been attending the church for some time. He always managed to slip out before Dick was able to get from the pulpit to the church door where he greeted and chatted with people after the service.

During some special evangelistic services, the man phoned Dick and, a little hesitantly, asked, "Would you and the evangelist visit my son who is in the Ontario Hospital at Whitby?"

Since the man had no car of his own, Dick and the evangelist picked him up and drove to Whitby. It was a silent trip. At the hospital, the three of them were admitted to the "Violent – Permanently Incurable" wing. They were taken to the locked room of a big, rusty-haired man of twenty-nine years. He was wary of them, and they could only pray with him and leave.

After the evangelistic services were over and the evangelist gone, Dick visited him several more times. He was able to talk with him a little, and prayed each time. Occasionally, he would get very violent and the attendants would protect Dick until he could get out.

During visits with the father of this twenty-nine-year-old inmate, Dick learned about this young man, Ross. He had been a rebellious child, stayed out of school, ran away, and was generally unmanageable by anyone. Finally, in one of his rages, he had attempted to kill his mother. They had him put away.

Almost every visit, Ross would ask Dick, "Get me out of this place." Dick would try to explain that he could not do so, then Ross would fly into a rage and accuse him, "You're on their side!"

meaning, of course, those who kept him locked up. The attendants were always nearby and protected Pastor Bombay from harm. It was all very nerve-wracking. Dick began to wonder if any good was being accomplished by the visits, talks, and prayer with Ross.

For almost a year and a half, Dick kept visiting, trying to talk and pray with Ross. One day, as they were on their way to visit Ross, Dick felt impressed to definitely speak to Ross about the salvation of his soul. He had already attempted this many times but without success, for often he would become violent.

As soon as they arrived that day, Ross insisted that Dick get him out of there. Dick recalled the question he asked him: "Ross, do you want to get out of here, or do you want to get rid of what put you in here?" He went on to explain what he meant, and then asked Ross if he understood. He said he did and that he wanted to be free from what made him like he was. This was his first positive response in one and a half years.

Dick had often asked if Ross would pray, but he never would. This day he asked Ross again if he would pray. Ross said, "I can't pray." He had never prayed and didn't know how. So, Dick had him repeat a prayer after him, fitted to Ross' need. He repeated every word.

They had been sitting opposite each other, and when Dick opened his eyes, he saw tears streaming down Ross' face. Ross opened his eyes and, with the back of his hand, wiped the tears away. He was smiling! Dick's heart leaped with joy. He asked Ross if he believed God had heard his prayer. Ross replied, "I *know* He did!" Then Dick asked him if he could tell him how he knew. Ross brushed his big hand across his chest and said, "I feel different in here!"

The next time they went to the ward to visit Ross, he was not there. They had moved him from the violent ward to cottage 13, which was the first step toward freedom. The next time he was in cottage 10, and the next visit he was mowing the lawn with other patients. Up until that time, he had never been allowed anything more dangerous than a spoon.

Two weeks later, his father called Dick again, and Dick said he would pick him up shortly and take him for another visit. There was a long pause, and Dick could hear the father weeping. Dick thought something drastic had happened, but when the father regained his composure, he said, "We don't have to go to the hospital anymore. Ross is sitting right here beside me at home."

Dick visited other patients in that hospital, and one day, Dr. Frazer, the Hospital Superintendent, asked him what he had done for Ross. Dick related simply that he had prayed with him and God had delivered him. Dr. Frazer said, "It must be so! We gave Ross seventy-eight shock treatments, and we might as well have attached the electrodes to the horns of a bull." His case had been considered hopeless. They had never had such a patient leave the hospital. "Except," as the doctor said, "when they were carried out in a coffin."

Other hospital attendants came to the church in Oshawa and told Dick that in all their experience they had never seen a similar case; it *must* have been God.

Ross could be found in church every Sunday. Before Dick left Oshawa, he baptized Ross, along with several others. Dick said, "It was like baptizing the man from the tombs in Gadara."

21

Dick, Money, and "Stuff"

In 1944, Dick and his family moved into a new neighbourhood, 152 Mill Street. It was in the College Hill district in Oshawa. Naturally, as a family, they wished to establish good relationships with their new neighbours. Most of them proved friendly, but one of their immediate neighbours proved to be not only unfriendly, but downright nasty. When Dick spoke to him, he would either ignore him completely or just mumble. This attitude carried over to his two sons who were bigger than the two Bombay boys, Dave and me. More than once they drove the two of us home frightened, beaten, and in tears because of the zeal of their dislike.

The whole Bombay family was distressed by all this, and Dick sought ways of "overcoming evil with good," but nothing worked. It became a matter of regular prayer, since this was a brand new experience for them. Almost a full year passed with no lessening of the tension and no change in sight.

One of the members of the church had a large strawberry patch and was going to build a house on it. He offered Dick as many strawberry plants as he wanted. Dick went with a few baskets and dug up more plants than he could possibly use, but, after all, the rest were going to be excavated and ploughed under. His garden space was limited, but since this was during World War II and nursery stock was very difficult to get, he took much more than necessary.

While Dick was planting his abundant supply of strawberry plants, he noticed his uncivil neighbour come out into his back yard with a shovel and a small tray of strawberry plants. Apparently, he had been successful in buying only a dozen plants.

Dick watched out of the corner of his eye as the neighbour kept surreptitiously looking over at the quite large patch of strawberries he was setting out. It was a slightly hungry look, and finally, he came over to the fence and, in a rather gruff voice, asked, "Where'd you get all the plants? I searched and searched, and all I could get was the dozen I just planted."

Dick told him how he had come to get his. The neighbour asked if he could go and get some too. Dick had to tell him that the whole patch had been excavated and chewed up in preparation for the foundation of the new house. The neighbour then offered to buy some plants from Dick.

Dick went back to his baskets, picked up one that was still full, handed it over the fence with the comment, "Help yourself. I've got more than I can use. And they're free, as many as you want." The neighbour thanked Dick, although not very warmly.

The strawberries were an "ever-bearing" variety, and it was not long before they were both picking a few. It was a good summer, and soon Dick and his neighbour were competing for the biggest and best. The next summer, they both had a bumper crop, and they ended up supplying the whole immediate neighbourhood.

Dick was like that all his life. He'd give, never expecting anything in return.

Dick often wished he could have won that neighbour to the Lord. But at least he had lost an enemy and found a friend. Even the boys of the two families became more friendly, and there were no more bloody noses in the Bombay brood.

They lived in peace and harmony until the church bought a manse into which the Bombays moved. And you'll never guess who not only offered but helped them move!

When You See Your Brother in Need

Dad often gave, and no one but Mom would know about it. My cousin Ken Bombay became privy to one of these long-lasting acts of giving when Dad asked him to check up on something. He then swore Ken to secrecy on the subject. We feel the secret can now be told, since both Dad and my uncle George have both gone to be with their Lord.

Uncle George had very little on which to retire. This was before P.A.O.C. pastors had much of a retirement plan, if any at all. Dad was to speak to this issue at General Conference, and because of his well researched and prepared presentation, a retirement plan was put in place. But it was too little too late for Dad's brother George.

Ken went to his father, the retired Rev. George Bombay, in the late 1970s. Ken asked the question Dad had told him to ask. He said, "Dad, have you been getting the $25.00 a month from the P.A.O.C. National Headquarter which has been anonymously designated for you as a gift?" Uncle George affirmed that he was receiving it, then asked a question of his own: "Ken, have you been sending that $25.00 every month?"

Ken said that it was not he who was sending it, and explained that he had promised never to reveal the source of that monthly gift.

Dad had always felt that George had experienced several tragedies in life, while Dad had only a few minor problems. George's son Doug was killed in a highway accident. His daughter Joyce died as a relatively young mother, from cancer, after having a leg amputation. George himself had lost an eye.

And there was another reason. George had sacrificed high school to work in the tannery, then a woolen mill, to help support the family, while Dad, the youngest, was given the opportunity to attend and graduate from high school.

He did not want George to know where the money was coming from because he didn't want George to be beholden to him or embarrassed in any way.

Again, giving without expecting or even wanting anything in return.

How Dick Became Rich

Dick had been born into a family that had always been plagued by poverty. We, his children, were never really aware of this, since we had a home full of love and care.

This poverty was not because his father, John, would not provide for them. He did the best he knew how. But, being a disobedient child of God for so many years, he could not rightly claim God's promise, "...whatever he does shall prosper!" (Psalm 1:3). Dick often heard his father say, "God is against me!"

When Dick's father was sixty-two years old, he finally turned to the Lord, and his last years were finally marked by freedom from indebtedness. They owned their small but modest house and were free from the grip of poverty. But they were never to become "well off" as a family.

When John became too old for active heavy work, he became

a night watchman in a lumber mill. One night, while all alone, he had a stroke but was able to crawl out to the street where the patrolling policeman found him and took him home. He had no idea that he had suffered a stroke. He was partially crippled after that and was able to walk only slowly with the help of a cane. At that time, Dick was pastoring the church in North Bay.

Dick would visit his father in Bracebridge as often as he was able, and on one occasion, Pa (all the children of the family called him 'Pa') asked Dick to walk with him back into the pine woods behind the house on Woodward Street. They could stand at the brow of the ravine and look down through the trees onto the beautiful Muskoka River. As they stood there under the trees, Pa said to Dick, "I am old now and cannot work any more. Dorothy (Dick's sister who lived at home still) pays us board. I have my old age pension, but your mother doesn't yet get hers. Dick, if you will come home and look after us, when we are gone, you can have this place. It's not worth much, but it's all we have."

Pa went on to talk about the hardships the family had endured, and how grateful they were that in their old age they would be cared for. Dick was in turmoil. It would mean that he would have to leave the ministry. He felt clearly gifted by God to spend his life in ministry. It had been confirmed by many others, including leaders in the churches. He did not want to disobey God. But he also remembered what the Bible said, "Honour your father and your mother, that your days may be long."

He also thought of the biblical instance where the young man thought he could escape the responsibility for his parents by making a vow and an offering. He was torn between the two. He wanted to do what was right toward God and toward his parents, and he could not honestly choose. In his heart, as he stood there, he asked God to show him what answer to give to his father, for he knew an answer was expected.

For quite a time they stood silently together in the trees. At last, Pa stretched out his tough old hand, placed it on Dick's arm and said, "Boy, forget what I have just said. When I was your age, God called me to the ministry. I did not respond to God, and you know the life I have lived and the troubles we have all had. I will not ask you to disobey God and suffer what I have suffered."

Dick knew precisely what Pa was talking about. He knew about the broken marriage before he was born. He knew the common-law relationship with his own mother out of which he was born. It was two years afterward that the death of his first wife allowed him to legalize his relationship with Dick's mother. All the children knew the embarrassment. Most of the children had been from Pa's second marriage with Nettie. He knew of the move from Southwestern Ontario into the North country to try to escape the local knowledge of his sin. But the reputation followed him.

The unfortunate fact is that Pa blamed Nettie for all his problems. But the real root of his problems was that he had turned his back on God's call into ministry. Living outside the will of God is the most uncomfortable place in the universe.

Dick knew about Pa being swindled out of the farm he had bought, and that everything was lost that time. He knew about Pa's best friend who had intercepted Pa's mail from England, and how the inheritance he should have received from the Old Country was side-tracked. He never saw a cent of that. It was a long and painful story. He tried to get right with God, but he saw no way to make things right with his first wife, nor knew what to do about the one who was eventually to become his second wife. But he did get soundly saved and right with God when he was sixty-two years of age. Now, he wanted to do what was right in the sight of God.

By this time, under those Muskoka pines, they were both weeping. Up to that point in his life, Dick had no idea that Pa had once felt called of God to the ministry. He certainly had many qualifications which would have fit him for ministry. He had a good singing voice. He was a very friendly man and was very well spoken, even though his formal education was limited. In his later life, he earned the respect of all who knew him, in spite of his past. He was able to lead many to the Lord who had lived lives such as his own former life.

It was Pa who made the decision he had asked Dick to make. "You follow the Lord, and He will take care of your mother and me."

All of the children had pitched in, and the balance owing on the house was paid off. Pa and Mother lived out their days in comparative comfort, with no more worries about money. Dick continued in the ministry. Dick's sister Dorothy inherited the house by common consent of the rest of the family, and that's where the matter lay for many years.

But life in the ministry in the late 1920s and '30s was not a very lucrative position. Dick and his family suffered, as many others did, often for the basic necessities of life. The Depression was into full swing, and many people knew poverty in those days.

However, it was during this time, 1935 to be precise, that Dick married Olive Sternall, and it wasn't long before a little family was "round the table": five of them. Times were still hard, and as the two older boys, David and Calvin, were entering high school in Oshawa, Dick lay awake one night wondering, "How can we ever make out with such a small income?" They lived modestly, but each week, the pay was all spent by the time the next one came. It was natural that high school and later education would add to the expenses. Those who were responsible for setting Dick's salary never did recognize the situation in which their pastor lived.

As he lay awake thinking of ways he might appropriately increase his income, Dick seemed to hear an inner Voice say, "Did I not promise that anyone who would leave father and mother, houses and lands, and all else, would receive an hundredfold and also everlasting life?" (Matthew 19:27-29).

Dick breathed a sigh of relief and went to sleep. It was 1952.

It was very shortly after this that he got a phone call from his sister Dorothy, who had inherited the small house in Bracebridge. She asked Dick if he wanted to buy it. Dick told her he had no money, not even enough for a down payment. He asked Dorothy if she could wait a while so he could try to see what he could do. She said she'd be able to wait a week for his answer.

As Dick lay the telephone down, the front door bell rang. It was an acquaintance from years before in North Bay, a school teacher, who had accepted a school near Oshawa and was boarding in town. Rather facetiously, Dick asked him if he knew where he could borrow some money. He went on to tell this old friend of the offer from his sister, and when Dick told him how much he needed, the friend said, "The man with whom I board lends money on mortgages. I'll call him right now and see what he says." And he did. When he hung up the phone, he turned with a grin to Dick and said, "He'll do it! And for that small amount he doesn't want to bother with a mortgage. Just get a friend to co-sign a note and you can repay him as you are able."

Dick bought the old homestead. With his two sons, Dave and me, he fixed it up and used it as a summer place during July and August. He rented it out for the rest of the year, which helped to pay off the loan.

The old pine trees were beginning to die, so Dick made lumber of them, used some for himself, and sold the rest. The cutting of those trees was almost the death of Dick. One of the larger trees began to roll downhill while Dick was standing on top of it. He tried as hard as he could to run over the log, rather than fall backward and be crushed. I will never forget that moment as long as I live. I was just fourteen. Dave and I watched in horror as finally

Dad lost the battle and fell under the rolling log as it continued to roll and bounce down the hill.

Fortunately, there was a slight depression, filled with small limbs and twigs, under Dad as he fell. Still, it almost crushed the life out of him. Dave and I were terrified as we watched it happen. Dad slowly and painfully struggled to his feet, and slowly climbed up the hill with our help. It was a slow and painful trip back to Oshawa in the old 1946 Chevrolet for Dad that day. And Dave and I were wide-eyed and worried all the way. Tough and wiry as he was, Dad never suffered any lasting effects.

Dad later built a cottage on the property, at the edge of the river, and many vacations were spent there with the family. The house was eventually sold, but an access was retained to get to the cottage. That property became Dad's first personal possession of any property.

At about the same time, a man in Oshawa was moving a house to make room for the new City Hall and Fire Station. Dick bought a lot on a street from the same man who was grading the land, before the prices went up. He then bought the little house for a pittance and moved it onto a high foundation. I can remember the big flatbed truck moving slowly down Simcoe Street South, while hydro wires were lifted or temporarily disconnected as that little white house was transported through Oshawa to its new foundation.

Dick asked the board of his church if he could put in some time for himself as long as it didn't interfere with his pastoral responsibilities. They agreed. Dad was very skilled in carpentry, and he built a small apartment into the lower level. He ended up with a two-family dwelling. By renting both, he soon paid off the money he had borrowed to buy the house and property. This was the second property Dad acquired.

Meanwhile, Dick had gone to Africa for a two-year assignment through the Pentecostal Assemblies of Canada. Missionary allowances being what they were, his savings were absorbed, and when he came back to Canada, he had no cash. The missions department had not yet repaid him for the loss of salary sustained while serving them overseas.

After nearly two years, he was finally reimbursed, and he used this money as a down payment on another bungalow which had already been converted into a duplex. He had made an unbelievably low offer on it, but, since it was the last property of an estate, the offer was accepted for a fast settlement. The rent was far more than was needed to pay off the low balance owing at a rate of 4.5%, and it was almost totally paid off when he left Oshawa. He had been elected Superintendent of the Eastern Ontario and Quebec Conference of the Pentecostal Assemblies of Canada.

Dick moved to Belleville, selling his two properties in Oshawa. With the proceeds he was able to buy a triplex in Belleville and carry a mortgage for about half the value of the triplex. Two other small debts on the triplex were paid off, and with the proceeds from the three rents, he was able to more than pay the mortgage payments. For the first time in his life, he was able to set aside some savings. He was fifty-five at the time, with two children, Lois and Richard Jr., still at home. David, myself, and Ruth were married and setting up our own homes.

Dick always had a caution about becoming too affluent. As a result, he had determined that when he reached a certain level in his finances, he would sell off all his properties and invest in Trust Certificates. All of his property dealings had not taken more than one or two hours per month in management and bookkeeping. There was no way he would let any of this stand in the way of his highest calling; the work of the ministry.

When he determined to resign from the Superintendency after nine years of continual service, Dick sold the triplex and had cash in hand within six months. At the same time, the District Executive offered him the Superintendent's cottage at Lakeshore Pentecostal Camp for what it had cost the District. Since Dick and his youngest son, Rick, had done most of the work in building it, the District leaders considered it a reimbursement for their labour. Dick retired from the Superintendency before he was sixty-three years old. Again, he was asked by the Missions Department if he would serve with them another two years, this time in Thailand. When they finished their job there, on schedule, they came back to Canada. On the day they arrived in Toronto, a message was waiting for them, which resulted in two delightful years of ministry with Pastor Don and Ardena Cantelon in Kingston Gospel Temple. They enjoyed those two last years of full-time ministry as much as any time, anywhere.

Finally, Dick retired in 1977. Well, almost retired!

At that time, Dick began to think about the promises of God, and the life of ministry and obedience he had lived. He wondered, "Did Jesus say those who followed Him would receive an hundredfold?" That's precisely what He did say, but did it come true?

As he thought over his life, after retirement, he remembered his father's proposal, and the decision his father had made. He was still unsure as to how he would have answered that question, but he knew where his heart was.

So, he did a little arithmetic. The property Pa would have given Dick was eventually sold to him by his sister. He sold that at a profit. He made a profit on each of his other properties, both in Oshawa and in Belleville, including another cottage he had built on Cashel Lake. When he added up the value of all his possessions, securities, car, cottage at Lakeshore Camp, furniture, etc., he came to the conclusion that it was far more than *one hundredfold*.

But, even more important to Dick was the wealth he had in friends – people who had been saved and helped through his ministry. He had fathers and mothers in the Gospel, with brothers and sisters innumerable. He had three sons and two daughters, yet many others considered him "father." Even his nephew, Ken Bombay, looked at Dick as one of only two possible choices for a "father" if his parents died prematurely. The other was Rev. Jack Lynn, one of Dick's friends, and a missionary for many years in Africa.

More precious than securities are the investments he and Olive have in Africa and Thailand and in many towns and cities across Canada. These are obviously not cashable at any bank, but they are "where moth and rust do not corrupt and where thieves do not break through and steal!"

Widow Food

When World War II was over, things began to return to normal. Wage and price controls were lifted, and the cost of living soared. It seemed labour was prepared to make up for lost wages during controls. All the wage earners in the church came home with fattening pay cheques, and church offerings rose accordingly.

Everyone but the pastor was prospering. There seemed to be no thought for him.

Dick, with his wife and four children, lived at a subsistence level. They had carried their share of the cost in a building program to accommodate their growing congregation. Dick kept thinking, "Surely the church board will make an upward adjustment of my salary," but nothing was ever said or done about it. Each week costs rose, and it was a subject on everyone's lips, but there was no corresponding increase for Pastor Bombay. He'd had a car since his days in North Bay, but without enough money to buy sufficient gas, he finally bought a bicycle to reduce the cost of travel, both in visiting, and to and from church.

In desperation, he finally brought the matter before the board of the church, and although there was money in the treasury, there seemed to be no corresponding sympathy in the board. He was not granted a raise. One particular board member seemed determined to keep the pastor's salary low based on the idea that this would cause the pastor to spend a good deal of time in prayer....

He did that in any case.

On Tuesdays, it was Dick's regular custom to visit several shut-ins and pensioners, members of the congregation, and minister to their spiritual needs, pray with them, and spend some time with them. He would often serve them communion.

Frequently, they would hand him money, and every time, he would ask them to which department they wished the money to go. He would mention Missions, the Radio Department, Sunday School, the General Fund or the Building Fund, or anything else. Dick always wrote down what they instructed him to do. On Sunday, he would turn it over to the treasurer of the church and tell him the source of each gift so that proper receipts could be issued. This had been done for several years, and not once had any of this money been directed to Dick, nor had he ever taken any for himself.

On the Tuesday, following the board meeting in which it was decided to refuse to grant an increase in salary, he made his usual shut-in calls. The first visit was to a partially crippled, retired gardener and his wife. With them lived an old friend, a spinster from England. All were Christians and supported the church according to their means for many years.

As Dick was leaving, the little wife pressed some money into the pastor's hand. As usual, he asked where they wished it to go. Her reply was startling, if only because it was such a departure from their usual designation. She said, "Daddy and I have been thinking and talking about you and your little family, and we would like you to keep this for yourself."

While this was going on, the spinster left the room but soon returned and also handed Dick some money. Again, Dick asked where it should be directed, and her reply was the same as the couple's. Obviously, they had been talking. Dick was astonished, but tremendously grateful.

The next call was a frail little old lady who was seldom able to attend church. When she gave him a few small bills, he asked her the usual questions, and to his complete surprise, she directed him to keep it for his own use. Dick was flabbergasted. This had never happened before!

Dick made three more calls to shut-ins that day. In every case, there was the same response to his question, "What do you want done with this?" Dick went home with more than a full week's salary. You can probably guess that his salary was not very big. Some years later, when he left that church, his salary was only eighty-five dollars a week, and the pastor following him received considerably more than that per week. He never made an issue of pastoral salary for himself.

Month after month, for almost a year after the board had decided not to grant a raise, this was repeated by the same people. In every case, and on every occasion, Dick asked the same question, "What do you want done with this money?" All of these people, unknowingly, were making up to Pastor Bombay what the board had refused to grant.

Almost a year later, when the board itself brought up the matter of his salary, they gave a modest increase. Dick was grateful, but he was convinced that the board and the church missed the blessings they would otherwise have experienced had they properly cared for their pastor.

Then a most remarkable thing happened. Each Tuesday Pastor Bombay continued to visit the shut-ins. Again they handed him money, and again he asked them the usual question. These people could not possibly have known of the increase the board had just granted, but each one in turn directed the money into various church departments. From that point on, he never received anything extra from them.

Dick often thought of the story in 1 Kings 17:9, and made the comparison:

> The brook dried up (the board?)
> The oil flowed (to meet his need)
> The barrel wasted not until...

Dick kept personal financial records all his life. When he totaled what had been given to him that year through specific designations, it was almost exactly equal to what the board of the church should have given him that same year. He also reported this fact to the board (for their edification, of course). I have often wished I was a fly on the wall to have seen the reaction of that board!

Dick learned through all this that God in reality *does* meet all his needs, even if the human end of things fail.

He's not sure the board learned anything at all through the situation.

He Could Have Been a Millionaire

Dick knew that from his salary as a minister he would never be able to set aside enough to have a home for his retirement. This led him to look for a way to supplement his income. An opportunity came to buy a small house to rent out (aforementioned), and from the rent, he hoped to pay for the house itself.

However, he had no down payment, so he confided in an old friend that he needed three thousand dollars for which he could return a mortgage. He already had the small lot onto which he could move the house.

Dick's friend took him to an old retired friend of his, introduced him, and stated his case. Mr. Gerrard was a farmer on the west side of Oshawa, and Gerrard Street is named after him in that city.

Mr. Gerrard was in bed with a serious heart condition when they visited him. His doctor had advised him to retire, give up the farm, and slow down in order to extend his life. After Dick explained the situation to him, Mr. Gerrard told them he had no loose money to lend at that time.

Then the two old friends chatted on for quite some time, while Dick sat back and simply listened.

After a while, Mr. Gerrard turned to Dick again and said something like this: "I have no money that I can lend. I have spent all my cash having the farm surveyed and sub-divided into building lots. I have already sold six lots at $600.00 each. I am keeping the farm house and the outbuildings and will continue to live here. There are ninety-five acres already to be sold. I am a church man and I know you preachers have very little opportunity to make and save money. So I am going to make you a proposal that I think you can handle." (He must have figured this all out while he and the other older man were chatting.)

He continued, "I will sell you the balance of the farm, ninety-five acres, and there are five lots to every acre, already sub-divided. That means there are four hundred and seventy-five lots to be sold. I do not need a down payment, and you can pay it off as the lots are sold. What would you think of that?"

For Dick to say he was astonished would be a great understatement. He did a little mental math and came up with a figure of $285,000.00. Up to that point, Mr. Gerrard had said nothing of his price, and Dick was too flabbergasted to ask. So Mr. Gerrard continued, "I want $12,500 for the ninety-five acres. As long as you agree to pay me each time you sell a lot, there will be no interest on the balance."

Dick's friend, who had introduced him to Mr. Gerrard, sat with *his* mouth open, but finally spoke and said, "Mr. Bombay, that is a wonderful bargain he has offered you, and I think you should accept it."

Dick was silent for quite some time, both astounded... and thinking. There ran through his mind what had happened to several ministers he knew; how they had become involved in business, and though they prospered financially, they grew lean in their souls and quit the ministry. Some left off following the Lord altogether, and in one case, his family broke up, ending in divorce. Many other thoughts rushed through his mind.

He knew he was just a human being, like those other men, and this could easily lead him down the same path that those others had gone. He admitted he was tempted. He had two sons about to enter high school, and three smaller children, and had often wondered how he could educate all of them on his meager income. Here was an opportunity for a way out. A big and easy way out!

He explained his dilemma in some detail to those two Christian gentlemen, and said he felt he would have to decline the offer. He told Mr. Gerrard that he was extremely grateful for his generous gesture.

After a pause, Mr. Gerrard said that he understood and that perhaps Dick had made the right decision.

They prayed together, and Dick left with his friend. He drove his friend home, and remembers only one remark he made, "I think that must have been a difficult decision, but perhaps you did the right thing."

Later, Dick learned from his friend that the price of the land soon increased to $1,200.00 per lot, and before the year ended, it had gone up to $2,000 for each lot. Then a developer bought all the remaining property, and today the entire farm is covered with houses valued at $200,000.00 each, or more.

Dick did not regret making that choice. God has been good, and his children have all been educated, married, and are prospering. His retirement was adequate for both Mom and Dad, and as Dick often said, "I'd rather have Jesus than silver or gold."

22

Dick – The Official

Dick was a man interested in the social and spiritual condition of not just his own church and denomination, but was also one of the earliest Pentecostal preachers to become involved in matters of civil concern.

During the Second World War years, while pastoring in Oshawa, Dick volunteered to be a warden in the city to help assure the readiness of the city for any war-related problem which might arise. I remember him putting on his arm band of identification at night and taking a walk through the streets of Oshawa to check that people were observing the "black-out" when it was required. I vaguely remember his being involved in the training of civilians for war-readiness and response, if anything should happen in the "Motor City" where some war vehicles were being built.

He had some mysterious association with "Camp X" on the

west side of Oshawa down near Lake Ontario. He seemed to have access to the camp, but never spoke about it other than to point it out to us as we would pass by its entrance, stating, "Never, ever disobey that sign on the gate." There was a strong warning on the sign, including the large lettered words, "No Entry!" All that was visible was tall radio antennae and the peeked roofs of a few scattered buildings. We suspected his access to "Camp X" had more to do with his ministerial qualifications than anything else. "Camp X" was where Canadians were trained in espionage.

A man with whom Dick would develop a close working relationship in District administration one day turned up, still in uniform after active service, at the end of the war in 1945. He was with his father, Rev. George Upton, who came to Oshawa to preach. The man was Gordon Upton, who remembered that day. He wrote:

"I was impressed by the warmth and friendliness of this pastor who seemed to 'have it all together.' Some years later, he drove an old 1937 Chevy, while most of his peers were driving much newer models, probably financed to the hilt. One day, when he was chided for still driving such an old car, Dick's response was simply, 'Well, mine's paid for.'"

When Gordon was in Bible College he was invited by Dick to come to preach in Oshawa. Although terribly sick with a severe throat infection, Gordon forced himself out of bed and went to Oshawa for the service. Gordon wrote about that day:

"After I had just begun preaching, my voice gave out totally, and I couldn't speak above a whisper. I was forced to sit down. It was a most embarrassing moment. Pastor Bombay rose to the pulpit and said, 'I believe that God can heal this man right now.' With that he laid his hands on me and prayed. My voice returned instantly, clear and strong, and I finished the message without any further problem."

Rev. Gordon Upton was to become Assistant Superintendent with Dick many years later.

Dick was also one of the few early Pentecostal ministers whose opinions and association with other ministers and denominations were not just congenial, but aggressively friendly. He was a member of the Ministerial Association in Oshawa and became perhaps the first Pentecostal minister in Canada to become chairman of such an interdenominational organization. Considering that in the late forties and early fifties, "Pentecost" was still considered somewhat of a "cult," this was quite an aberration from the norm throughout most of North America.

Not all ministers in Oshawa accepted him, and, in fact, one pastor wrote a rather harsh booklet which condemned the Pentecostal teachings, entitled *Light vs. Darkness*. Darkness, of course, was the matter of "speaking with other tongues" and several other Pentecostal distinctives. It was interesting to note that the pastor who was so much against Dick and the growth of Pentecostal Churches in Oshawa had a sudden change of heart.

The good Reverend had visited his son in California where he was convinced to actually attend a Pentecostal service in an Assemblies of God church there. In the process, he was "filled with the Holy Ghost, speaking with other tongues." He arrived early on a Sunday morning at Dick's office door at Simcoe Street Pentecostal Church, and rather contritely asked for the privilege of speaking to Dick's congregation. After some hesitation, Dick decided to give him the pulpit. The former enemy of Pentecost gave witness to his experience with God, apologizing and asking the forgiveness of Dick and the congregation for his former attitude and actions.

After his many years in Oshawa, Dick became the "dean" of pastors in Oshawa. Other pastors and ministers of various denominations would seek his counsel.

District Superintendent

When Dick returned from Kenya, he returned also to pastor the church in Oshawa which had given him a two-year leave of absence. In those years, he also served as Assistant District Superintendent to Rev. Wilbur Greenwood, which was largely a standby position in the event that the Superintendent became indisposed.

During a District Conference, before he was Superintendent, Dick had been instrumental in pushing for unemployment benefits for ministers. This was before going to Thailand. He went well prepared, with all kinds of documentation, using his own case as an example. He accomplished his purpose. Unemployed ministers, at that time, could not get unemployment benefits.

At a conference in Ottawa, he had discovered there was a large amount of money in the Minister's Pension Fund. He had done his research well, and when he called for a rise in benefits, he was roundly applauded. Immediately after that conference, the fund was adjusted properly.

In 1964, only two years after his return from Thailand, Dick was elected as Superintendent of the Eastern Ontario and Quebec Conference of the Pentecostal Assemblies of Canada. The conference took place in Scarborough that year.

Rev. Gordon Upton, who worked closely with Dick, wrote about his association with Dick.

"He was never one to be influenced by peer pressure. He was a "meat and potatoes" man, no flair or pomp. He was just a hard worker whose life had been tempered by having to do a man's work in his youth. This helped to forge his solid work ethic. He exercised firm but loving discipline with his children, all five of whom have grown to be a credit to him and a blessing to the Kingdom of God. These same characteristics he carried through every phase of his ministry.

"For some time, he served as Director of Children's Ministry for the District of Eastern Ontario and Quebec. Among other things, this involved responsibility as the Director of the Boys' and Girls' camp at Cobourg.

"The boys were billeted in accommodations above the dining hall, now known as 'The Gables.' On one particular night, the boys would simply not settle down, and at midnight, they were still carrying on. His solution to the problem was to get them all up and dressed and run them around the dining hall until their tongues were literally hanging out. Then he sent them back to bed, and sleep overtook them all."

I personally happen to know the truth and have the vivid memory of that event, because I, as one of Dick's sons, was one of the culprits.

While Dick was Superintendent of the Eastern Ontario and Quebec District of the Pentecostal Assemblies of Canada, he had great burdens for both Quebec and the Northlands of both provinces.

He would often speak to us of his family with a certain amount of pride in the fact that he was not just English in his background, but could trace a part of his ancestry back to aboriginal North American Indian as well. Certainly he seemed at his happiest moments when he was in the northland in the bush, in God's natural creation. I've seen it. His familiarity with the bush, the trees, the wind, and the total lack of the intrusions of buildings, machines, and unnatural noises seemed to set his soul at ease. He loved the freedom of nature's wild, both flora and fauna.

But nature can be a bit difficult at times.

On one occasion, he was, in his position as District Superintendent, travelling to northern Quebec from Ottawa. In his company were two men, Rev. Robert Argue, National Director of Home Missions, and Rev. Dick Zabriskie. The first part of the trip was warm and sunny. The hardwood forests stretched out in the distance. Dick called it "a riot of colour."

A service was planned for Senneterre. They drove through Chapais and then on toward their ultimate destination, Mistassani, on the north shore of the lake by the same name. Miles of road passed under their wheels as they pushed on.

It had been raining heavily in that area for several days, and before they left the paved road, the rains began again. Some spots became so difficult that they had to detour around some small wash-outs. Then the road disappeared altogether. The car would go no further, and they were at least four miles from their goal.

They left the car, shouldered their packs, and began the trek toward the Indian Village. They were soon drenched, and their rubber boots were filled with muddy water. Darkness came. In some parts, where there was still some trace of the road, green poles had been laid out, but they slanted toward the gutter full of water. More than once their boots simply slid down the poles, landing them more than knee deep in a water-filled trench. At other times, their boots were suctioned into oozy clay soil, this too finding place inside their boots. They had little choice now but to go ahead.

When they finally did arrive in the village, it was pitch black, and they were suddenly surrounded by a large pack of barking and snarling dogs. They fended them off and, from the people who were aroused by the commotion, they sought directions to the home of the missionary, Marcia McCorkle.

On such a night, and in such a condition, there was no hope of holding a service. Miss McCorkle settled for the night in a neighbour's hut, and the three men settled in Marcia's hut.

By morning, the rain had quit and the sun was shining, but there was plenty of water to wash bodies, socks, and inside their rubber boots. Because the supply trucks with the winter supplies had not been able to get in for some time because of the weather, and the boats had not yet arrived, they ate what was available: huge portions of lake trout, and an apple each.

After holding their meeting, including public services and meetings with the church leadership, they had to get back to their car. They knew that getting back would be no easier than their trek to get there. Arrangements were made with the Hudson's Bay Fur Company to rent a freight canoe with an outboard motor. An elderly Indian employee was to be their navigator, engineer, guide, and general expert.

It looked ominous. In the distance and slightly ahead, threatening thunder heads were rising. Their guide kept the canoe weaving through a string of small islands, heading for the point nearest to where their car had been left.

Suddenly rain burst on them, and they crouched under a large plastic sheet in the bottom of the large canoe. Water drained off the sheet and rained into the boat until they were sitting in it, and they were soon drenched again. The wind began to rise, and the lake began to become choppy. Dark, black clouds were coming and appeared to be ready to pass across their path through the water.

The guide himself slid down into the bottom of the canoe and began to fight the rising waves. When they came out from the shelter of the islands, real trouble began. Water was coming into the canoe from both sides. The wind whipped up white caps, and they saw a huge wave cutting across their bow.

The guide threw caution to the wind, put the motor on full power, and told the three men to get down as low as they could in the canoe. He headed straight for shore, trying to race the wave, but it kept gaining on them. They prayed, as anyone in their right mind would do!

The wave caught the canoe just as it headed up onto the shore, and carried it up past the shore and into the bush. Everyone scrambled out and hauled the canoe further onto the shore to keep the receding wave from carrying it back into the lake. As they looked out on the lake, it was thrashing in a fury that made them feel like it was angry that they had escaped.

They fished their sodden packs out of the canoe, then helped to turn the big canoe over on the slope leading back to the shore where, when the wind and fury stopped, their guide could get it back into the lake. The last they saw, as they trudged away, was their guide settling in under the overturned canoe to wait out the storm.

There just happened to be a path leading in the general direction of the road, and they took it. To their surprise and delight, the car was in sight, in the direction they needed to drive home. Soggy and tired, they turned the car around and headed south.

Dick wrote, "We knew that, had the big wave caught us before we reached shore, we would surely have foundered. All of us were in heavy clothing which would have dragged us down into the near-freezing water. We gave thanks together to God for deliverance, but it was an experience none of us would care to repeat."

100 Huntley Street

As District Superintendent of the Eastern Ontario and Quebec District of the Pentecostal Assemblies of Canada, Dick's duties involved many, many areas of responsibility beyond the oversight of the churches in his own district. By virtue of his office, he was a member of the General Executive of the P.A.O.C. which involved membership on various committees. And there were *ad hoc* duties as well.

A young preacher named David Mainse had begun using television early in his ministry. It had grown to become national in its reach and influence. David Mainse was also pastoring a growing church in Sudbury, Ontario, and his time and the church resources were being stretched to keep both the church and the television ministry moving forward. Dick, along with others, became involved.

David Mainse writes of that time and development:

"Dick's brother George was my pastor when I made my life commitment to serve Christ. George was an evangelist who succeeded in encouraging us all to spend time at the altar of the church. Along the way, I heard of another Bombay family. The other Bombay was an excellent Bible teacher and pastor in Oshawa, Rev. Dick Bombay.

"I met his son Cal in Bible College. Then I really began to hear the stories, not just from Cal, but from the college teachers and from other students (from Oshawa). The general consensus was that Dick was a wise and compassionate pastor who, while pastoring one church in Oshawa, started several other churches in and around the city. He encouraged great church growth by a strong evangelistic effort and by encouraging his own church members to become members of the new congregations. I thought, 'What a Christ-like visionary – an example of what a pastor should be!'

"My most memorable experience, however, came after Dick had been elected by his fellow ministers as District Superintendent for Eastern Ontario and Quebec of the P.A.O.C. By this time, I was serving in Western Ontario as pastor in Sudbury. Crossroads Television had been on-air weekly since 1962 and was seen in most Canadian cities. My local church board was concerned about the heavy load of financial responsibility which the television ministry placed on the congregation.

"The 1966 General Conference had formed a National Radio and Television committee in order to smooth the path for local churches that were ministering via the media in cities other than the one in which they were located. I think I may have been the main reason for this. Rev. Don Feltmate, the first pastor in Southern Ontario who had invited me to minister in his Oshawa church, was chairman. He pastored King Street Church, one of the churches mothered by Dick Bombay. Other members of the committee were Rev. Tom Johnstone, General Superintendent, Rev. Don Emmons, Superintendent of Western Ontario District, and Dick Bombay.

"I'll never forget the heroic efforts of these four men as they drove 300 miles north in a snow storm to meet with my church board and me. I still remember the wise counsel of Dick Bombay as he assured the church board that the 'child,' Crossroads TV, could be moved onto a strong national foundation, both legally and financially. It happened, just as Dick said it could.

"By that time, Cal had been in Africa for four years already. Little did I know that by the end of the century Cal and I would have worked on the same Crossroads team for twenty years.

"I've been very conscious that Dick Bombay continues to influence us strongly by his deposit of faith, wisdom, and plain common sense which he left in our lives."

The Quebec Connection

As District Superintendent, Dick's responsibilities included the co-ordination and relationships between the French-peaking and the English-speaking churches in Quebec. He had a general oversight of the French Conference and worked very closely with the leadership.

He was asked to be the main speaker at the French P.A.O.C. winter convention. At the same time, there was an evangelist who was troubling the churches in Quebec with what he called, "The Word of Knowledge." He would name a disease during a service, and when and if someone acknowledged that they had such a disease, the evangelist would tell them they were healed. He never waited for any acknowledgement that the healing had actually taken place. When it became known that the evangelist was acting immorally, he was basically rejected by the churches. So he began his own church in Montreal.

Following one of the afternoon sessions in the convention, this topic became the subject of conversation. There were about thirty-two people present in the discussion, including ministers and their wives. Dick had not touched on this vexing question, but during the conversation was asked what he thought about this so-called "Word of Knowledge."

It just so happened that Dick had read a medical article concerning the frequency of human ailments. A sore back led the list, with others following in order of frequency. He tried to remember the order before he answered.

Dick said, "I am not going to answer your question directly, but I would like to give you a demonstration." He went on to say, "There is someone here with a sore back between the shoulders and pelvis." The response was immediate. Mrs. Bergeron, wife of the Superintendent of the French Conference, raised her hand, saying that she had suffered much and for a long time.

Dick named another ailment and got a similar response from someone else. He was doing so well that he named another ailment with the same response again. By this time, there was some consternation, because they suspected that Dick too was exercising the "Word of Knowledge."

Dick did not want to deceive them, so he explained about the article he had read. He explained that it would probably be common knowledge, since the article had appeared in the popular monthly magazine, *Reader's Digest.* He suggested that perhaps some of these "healers" had read it also and were capitalizing on it. On the other hand, they may have had pure motives, and if the pain of an individual was pointed out, it may, by suggestion, help them to believe that God was about to heal them. In fact, many healings were reported, especially by the "healer"....

Dick was quick to add that "God indeed is sovereign and may use many means to quicken the faith of His suffering saints. Such means are allowable... providing the motive and method are honest."

He went on to point out that they should take note that many of these "healings" by the "healer" were only so in his mind.

Then There Was the Tabernacle Bell

As District Superintendent, it was his responsibility to manage the Lakeshore Pentecostal Camp. He had been involved in the very beginning of the camp when it started in 1936, while he pastored in nearby Cobourg. He had a hand in the beginning of another major camp called Braeside Camp, while he filled in for J.H. Blair in Hamilton who founded the camp.

The Lakeshore Campground has been popular since its beginning. I can recall my own youth and the summers I spent there. Many young people would spend a week or more with their parents enjoying the beautiful lakefront, meeting friends, and attending meetings and various special events.

But there were rules – particularly for the "unruly" youths. Some forbidden activities included such things as slamming the shutters over the windows on cabins in the middle of the night. Other times a blood-curdling scream would be heard and, of course, no reason for it to be found.

Another of the more tempting possibilities was the ringing of the tabernacle bell – in the middle of the night. One night, Paul Willoughby, aged fourteen, and Jack Richards, both to become ministers of the Gospel, were sitting comfortably with a few of their friends in Jack Richards' father's cottage. Just after midnight, the tabernacle bell began to ring. Someone was at it again.

This touched off the brilliant idea with Paul and Jack that they should elevate themselves momentarily to the position of Camp Cops. They took off with Paul's twin, John, and Nolan Swartzentruber to chase and try to apprehend the "evildoers." Whether or not they were truly trying to keep the peace, or were in fact envious that someone else got there first, could perhaps be debated.

Meanwhile, Dick Bombay had taken the camp speaker, Paul Olson, with a few others, into Cobourg for a late and final meal of that week of camp meetings. While the four young fellows were racing back and forth chasing the bell ringers, Dick and his car load, on their return from Cobourg, caught sight of running kids in the headlights. Dick took up pursuit of the pursuers. Now, these would be "camp cops" were being chased by the real camp cop, the District Superintendent and Camp Manager, Dick Bombay, who for some reason had a reputation as a very stern man.

Paul and John, thinking they had eluded Dick, were just coming up from the shore near the camp caretaker's office, when suddenly Dick shouted to Walter Perry, the camp caretaker, "Call the Provincials" (Police). Without much warning, Dick had a bear-hug on John Willoughby, and the others stood by meekly. They, together with Walter Perry, who was dressed comically in pajamas and rubber boots nearby, heard stern words from Dick. "You will be in my office this morning at 10:30!"

All four arrived on time, subdued and scared. Dick did have a reputation for strictness. They had no idea what the penalty would be. They stood before Dick, together with the whole camp committee. Dick, looking at them sternly, asked, "Do you boys realize the gravity of this situation?"

Silence.

Then Dick grinned, and the whole committee broke out in laughter. The committee session had already been planned in any case, and Dick laughingly said, "OK, boys, don't let it happen again."

Paul Willoughby said it was a turning point in his fourteen year old life. Dick Bombay had just given them permission to be teens, and in the process, prompted Paul to follow the Lord more closely. For years, every time Paul and Dick would meet, the memory of the summer of 1966 would cause them both to smile. Balance – rules without humour is deadly!

The Deacon With the Last Word

Dick travelled a great deal throughout the churches of Eastern Ontario and Quebec when he was District Superintendent (Bishop) in the Pentecostal Assemblies of Canada. In the process, he met hundreds of men who had been elected to official boards of churches. At times, he was filled with amazement and saddened at some who were elected. Some were so far below the standard set in God's Word (1 Timothy 3:1-13) that he had cause to wonder: Who had nominated them? How did they every achieve election? Fortunately, this was the exception, not the rule.

In the more than sixty years Dick gave to the ministry, he had the privilege of working with some of the greatest Christian gentlemen the P.A.O.C. has produced.

In one church he had pastored himself, he soon learned that the senior man who had served the most years on the church board had somehow become the "court of last resort." This man seldom entered a discussion, but when a motion was put forward, very often another member of the board would say, "What do you think, Brother?" (and he named the deacon). Then this deacon would come to life and either destroy what seemed to have already been agreed upon, or he would add his blessing. Naturally, he enjoyed this kind of recognition, but it was often most disconcerting to the other members. There were times when good and sensible decisions were hindered by his "veto."

Just such an occasion arose when they were in the middle of a building program and had to make some quick decisions for the next day's work to go ahead unhindered. When Pastor Bombay put the question for vote to the board, someone said, "I think we should hear what Brother (naming the deacon) has to say!"

Dick was in a quandary. How could he correct this situation without injury to a good brother? Suddenly, the answer came to him. He said, "We have had a full discussion and everyone has had opportunity to express himself, including Brother (the deacon with the last word). Don't you think it is unfair to place on him so much responsibility in making the final decision when all of you are expected to vote?"

There was a short silence and then Dick turned to the deacon and asked, "Would you care to make this decision yourself, or would you rather I should put the question to vote now?"

Without hesitation or offense, the deacon promptly replied that he had often thought too much responsibility was thrust on him by this means, and he would far rather that each should vote as he saw fit.

Those on the board, including Pastor Bombay, were saved from what had become an embarrassment and also an irritant to everyone who served with him.

That deacon was on the board when Dick arrived and remained for many years. He was a good man, and his name always stood at the head at election time. He probably served continuously on a board longer than any man in any of the P.A.O.C. churches across Canada. It was forty-nine years before he voluntarily retired because of his advanced age. Thank God for men like Brother "What's-his-name"!

The Death of the Righteous

At his retirement, Brother Crook and his wife moved into rooms in the home of their married daughter. Shortly after, he became ill. It turned out to be cancer of the stomach. When they operated on him, they found the cancer so wide-spread that it was impossible to remove through surgery. He was sent home to die.

Late one evening, the daughter phoned Dick and told him the doctor had just left and had made the statement that her father would probably pass away within the hour. She asked if Pastor Bombay would come.

When he arrived at the home, the whole family had gathered in the room, including two grandchildren. It was a sombre group, as they stood silently around the bed. The impending presence of death reduces even thoughts to whispers.

There was little appearance of life. His pulse was a feathering, occasional thing. Coldness had already set in, and as Dick took one cold hand in his, he repeated the Name, "Jesus," over and over again as the family stood around the last flickering of life. This went on for some time.

Suddenly, Brother Crook's hand began to close in a grip around Dick's hand. Colour came into his face, and his eyes flew open. He dropped Dick's hand and raised both of his own hands high, sitting up in bed at the same time. Then he began to speak. "I see Jesus. Look, don't you see Him? He's right there," he said, pointing. Then he turned and looked at each individual in the room, and asked the same question of each, "Can't you see Him?" No one else could.

Brother Crook continued to look at and talk to Jesus. He began to praise Jesus for His goodness. The family was astonished, but thrilled and happy at what was happening. Only Brother Crook himself and his wife were Pentecostal, and "Mother" was not the least surprised.

As he quieted and relaxed again, those around the bed laid him back on his pillow as he slipped back into a coma. But his breathing was strong and regular now. It was several days before he finally took his leave of this world and slipped into the presence of the Lord he loved and served for so many years.

At the memorial service in the church, Dick chose as his text,

Numbers 23:10:

"Let me die the death of the righteous and let my last end be like his."

Another responsibility as District Superintendent was to serve on the Board of Governors of Eastern Pentecostal Bible College. He was involved even before his elevation to office. Gordon Upton wrote:

"Dick had a keen interest in the training of young people for ministry. He served on the Board of Governors for twenty-five years. He began in 1948 while the college was still in Toronto. He was very active in the selecting of the site and the relocation of the college to Peterborough in 1952. He was elected Chairman of the Board in 1964 and continued through until his retirement from the District Superintendency in 1973.

"During those years," Gordon wrote, "I was closely associated with him, first as Presbyter, then later as Assistant District Superintendent. It was through these contacts that I came to know Dick Bombay quite intimately. He was a man of unblemished character and high ideals. He never flinched from an unpleasant task and never lost his cool even under extreme times of pressure. He was an able Chairman both of conferences and the executive meetings. He dealt with people firmly, but fairly, and was greatly appreciated and loved by his entire constituency. He was endowed with a special measure of wisdom and always had sound advice when it was needed.

"Through it all, he had a keen sense of humour. He often had a humourous story to tell, either from some incident which he had experienced, or a joke from one of his sons who seemed to keep him well supplied. He had one pet peeve. If a song leader would say, as they often did, 'Let's stand and change our position,' he would respond: 'How can you stand and not change your position?'

"Dick Bombay left an indelible stamp on the city of Oshawa, where he pastored for twenty-four years, and on the entire Fellowship of the Pentecostal Assemblies of Canada, which, under God, he served so faithfully for many years. Having known this man for more than fifty years, and following him through many facets of ministry, I have an immense appreciation for him. He was always known as a man who 'called a spade a spade' and was consistently forthright in his approach to both people and situations."

Gordon Upton continues: "Dick Bombay was among the last of a dying breed of pioneers who grew up through the privations of the early years of the last century which put iron in their souls and made them immune to the temptations of ease, materialism, and pleasure. He has not been forgotten among us. He left a legacy which successive and future generations can build upon. We are much the better for him having passed our way!"

One time, as Dick was on his way to Winnipeg to attend a General Conference with his Assistant District Superintendent, who was Rev. Roy Upton at that time, they were stopped by a policeman for speeding. Dick never seemed to be at a loss for words, and his response to the policeman was, "Sir, I am the Bishop of Eastern Ontario and Quebec, and my assistant is with me. We are travelling to attend a church conference in Winnipeg and would appreciate it if you would allow us to proceed." The officer replied, "Go ahead, but be careful. You look after the souls, and I'll look after the heels!"

Dick was an astute businessman, a faculty which served well while he was in office. When he came to office in 1964, the District Office also served as home to the former District Superintendent, Rev. W.B. Greenwood. The District was growing rapidly and more space was needed for offices for additional staff. Funds were rather scarce. He negotiated the sale of the house, bought a triplex apartment building, and moved the District Office into the centre apartment. The rent from the other two apartments paid off the mortgage, at no cost to the District.

Assistant General Superintendent

While serving as District Superintendent, Dick was also elected as Assistant General Superintendent in Winnipeg in 1966. One of the great Canadian men of God with whom he worked was Rev. Tom Johnstone, the General Superintendent of the P.A.O.C. Tom Johnstone, at age ninety-seven, had this to say about Dick as an official of the P.A.O.C. and as a friend:

"Dick Bombay, in the best and true sense, was an individualist. It was his nature. And he lived according to that 'new' nature which he acquired when he entered into that saving relationship with God through Jesus Christ. He was a compassionate believer who manifested the reality of his new birth to a degree in which I have seen in very few other people.

"He was rich in his relationships with anyone and everyone. He had the happy faculty of being able to minister to everyone as equal. To him, all people were equal. There was no such thing as one person being of more value than another. Wherever he ministered he had a remarkable cross-section of the community, regardless of their status in society, their colour, their language, or their peculiarities. Dick was never turned off by anyone. Everyone was a prospect for the New Birth into the First Family of the universe."

When Tom Johnstone was asked, "Did Dick Bombay ever back away from a touchy situation?" he snorted, "Never! But Dick was very thoughtful... did a lot of praying... spent a lot of time alone with God. Aside from the world's wisdom, he would be alone with God, seeking guidance, direction, and help. Thus, whether he was ministering to a pauper, a casual acquaintance on the street, or the wealthy, he had answers. He was a great soulwinner... bright... sharp!"

Tom Johnstone said of Dick and his involvement in executive and committee meetings: "He was a listener! He rarely jumped in with the first word. He listened, and listened carefully... judged wisely... and generally entered into the discussions only when he had thought the matter through. And when he spoke, he'd give the strong impression that he knew what he was talking about, and he did. He also lived in a way that backed up his declared thoughts and opinions."

David Mainse once asked Tom if Dick Bombay was a man worth knowing. Tom's answer was immediate and emphatic: "HO! If you were privileged to be a friend of Dick Bombay, you were a fortunate man! As General Superintendent, I had no problem going to Dick when I needed advice. Nobody would ever learn what I had talked about with him, or even that I had talked with him. He gave good counsel. He was one of my treasured counsellors during the time I was General Superintendent.

"When dealing with younger ministers, and knowing I needed another counsellor's help, I knew I could count on Dick to talk with them when I didn't have an answer. He never let me down. And he kept confidences. I loved that man as a trusted friend and fellow preacher. He never let me down."

When Tom knew this book was being written, he told me, "Cal, be sure to get your mother in there, too. She was as good a woman as he was a man, and... well, I loved them both! Had good reason to!"

Another man with whom Dick had close and long-lasting friendship in ministry was Rev. H.H. Barber, pastor for many years of Calvary Temple in Winnipeg, Manitoba. Rev. Barber writes of Dick, "There was an affinity of spirit between 'Dick' Bombay and myself in spite of the disparity in our ages. His central motivation was his love for the Scriptures and his hunger to reflect the likeness of Christ in every word, deed, and relationship."

Dick enthusiastically approved of the commitment by Rev. H.H. Barber to expository preaching combined with impassioned evangelism. Dick had invited 'Herb' to speak at Lakeshore Pentecostal Camp in the late fifties, and from that time, they were fast friends. Then, in 1962, when Herb was elected to become a "presbyter at large" to serve on the General Executive of the Pentecostal Assemblies of Canada, they began to know each other at the level of national governance.

Rev. H.H. Barber writes, "I learned to respect his clear-eyed objectivity, his gentleness with people combined with unflinching loyalty to principle, his quick mind, and his ability to express his convictions with clarity."

In those years, Dick, as District Superintendent, often invited Herb, his friend and very effective preacher, to speak at both District Conferences and Lakeshore Camp, and at other church events.

Rev. Barber wrote, "However effective Richard Bombay was as an administrator at District and National levels, I knew that he was primarily a pastor. He loved his flock. The needs of people gripped his heart. No doubt that is a prime reason we understood each other so well. I think he was one of the few who heartily approved of my life-long insistence on avoiding election to full-time administrative work due to my conviction that the 'rightest' calling God can give a man is to entrust him to be pastor, at the local level, of the flock of God.

"Richard Bombay did not have the privilege to procure as much formal education as some. But he was an avid reader and a life-student. His knowledge of the best in English literature, his rich vocabulary, and his careful adherence to grammatical accuracy impressed me. He was a man of broad interests, a keen student, and a quick learner in the school of experience.

"My friend Dick Bombay was unimpressed by the specious arguments which insist we must adopt the culture of our times if we hope to win our generation to Christ. He knew that you do not win the world by ape-ing the world. He had a God-given ability to discern between the clean and the unclean. Compromise was, to him, a dirty word."

When H.H. Barber wrote a controversial article published in the Pentecostal Testimony, the official organ of the P.A.O.C., about "rock music" in the church, he stirred up a firestorm. Finally, the editor called a total halt to all the letters to the editor about it.

Dick wrote directly to Herb Barber, commending him on his strong biblical stand. Dick referred to a comment he had made in the presence of such music in a church, which was presented in "the idiom of the World's St. Vitus Dance music." "We send missionaries to get people saved from the very thing we are welcoming into our churches," Dick wrote. His convictions were strong – very strong.

Herb Barber further wrote, "One day we happened to be browsing together through a Christian bookstore. Dick opened a copy of J.B. Phillip's paraphrase of the Bible to 1 Corinthians 14 and pointed out that Phillips had taken the liberty to alter the King James Version rendering that 'tongues are for a sign not to believers but to unbelievers' to the reverse, that tongues are a sign to believers, not unbelievers.

"A careful comparison of the statements preceding and following that passage shows that unbelievers may well consider tongues speakers to be mad.

"Richard Bombay was honest enough to risk the danger of being disloyal to distinctive Pentecostal teaching if it became a choice between exegetical fidelity and uncritical repetition. He loved the Word of God."

Herb Barber said, "It is an honour for me to write these words as a tribute to a dear friend. He was generous to those who disagreed with him. He was a spiritual giant. He was also practical enough to encourage young preachers to plan carefully for the material security of their families.

"He made the city of Oshawa one of the most Pentecostal cities in Canada by church planting. And then, when most men are ready to put their feet up and rest, he gave years of energy and devotion to missionary service on two continents.

"I cannot think of Richard Bombay without also thinking of the queenly lady who stood by his side through the years. The Bombays modelled what every marriage should be. Their hospitality and the warmth of their hearts provided all of us who knew them with cherished memories.

"We are all the richer because Richard and Olive Bombay passed our way on the highway to the Celestial City."

23

Dick – The Missionary

Kenya

Dad was always a man of both prayer and action. Mom was too, her prayer taking place behind the bedroom door and most of her action around the home. Occasionally she went visiting with Dad, particularly if "something didn't feel right" with Dad. She was also a first class pianist for congregational singing or accompanying singers. The perfect pastor's wife and a wonderful mother to boot – in the right sense.

Dad was also very open to other people's needs, opinions, and suggestions. He would often repeat the phrase, "I don't care who gets the credit, as long as God gets the glory!"

A need arose.

Urgent word had come from Nairobi, Kenya, telling of the great need for a multi-racial meeting place to be built. This came about because of some tent meeting held almost in the centre of Nairobi. The results of the meeting were dramatic, to say the least. Hindus, Muslims, Europeans, and African people had responded. Many were converted to Christ, and many were healed.

The P.A.O.C. Missions Committee, of which Dick was a member, was called to a special sitting to consider the need and to implement a response. They felt they needed a man with leadership ability, but also one who had experience building churches.

It became apparent that if the Mission was to capitalize on the blessing that had been poured out during the tent meeting, careful haste was needed. About $40,000 would be needed to provide at least a modest building. Their chief concern, though, was getting the right man to lead it.

Many names were considered. Eventually, three names were decided upon. They would be contacted and the proposal put to them in the following order: Mark Buntain (eventually famous for the Calcutta Mission of Mercy in India), Bob MacAlister (a noted evangelist and pastor), and Roy Upton (another solid and established pastor/teacher).

While the committee was still in session, each was contacted by telephone and, for a variety of reasons, none was available at that point to go to Kenya. The search continued.

All this while, Dick felt a growing conviction that he was, himself, the man to go. He shared this with no one, but sat with a pounding heart while name after name was proposed, but none was agreed upon as being suitable to the challenge. Dick wondered what the outcome would be. They seemed to have come up against a brick wall.

Without any preamble, a very close ministerial friend of Dick's, Rev. George Griffin, who sat right across from Dick at the committee table, spoke, pointing his finger at Dick, "There is the man we should send!"

Obviously, no one else had thought of Dick. Quickly, his capabilities were discussed by the others on the committee as Dick listened. "He has had church building experience." "He knows how to handle money." "Dick gets along with everyone, so getting along with the Kenya missionary staff would be no problem." In fact, some were either close friends (Jack and Edna Lynn) or missionaries who had gone out to Kenya from his church in Oshawa (Arn and Elsie Bowler). Many other points were discussed.

Dick sat quietly listening to himself being dissected. Finally, it was agreed that Dick should be asked if he was willing to go!

Dick had been doing a lot of thinking himself. He was pastor of a church that was still growing and planting new churches. What about his wife and three children who were still at home? David was married and working with Bell Canada. Cal was about to both graduate from Bible College and get married, with Dick, his father, officiating.

But when Dick was faced with the direct question, "Will you go?" he responded immediately and without reservation, "Yes."

It was agreed that Dick would receive regular missionary support while on the field in Kenya, but that when he returned, he would be recompensed in the amount between the missionary allowance and the salary he was currently receiving from his pastorate in Oshawa. (This commitment was only partially carried out several years later.)

After all the discussion was completed, the meeting adjourned. Dick drove home to Oshawa, wondering how to break the news to his family, especially Olive, and of course, the church. He thought neither would be easy.

Mom met him at the door. Dad greeted her, took her into his arms, and held her closely. This was no new thing. Dad was very open in his affection for Mom. We kids often watched the exchange of a kiss, a pat, a hug.

Dad was always one to "cut to the chase," so without any explanation whatsoever, he asked Mom, "How would you like to go to Africa for two years?" Without hesitation, Mom replied, "Where you go, I go!" Ruth, Lois, and Rick were caught between excitement and foreboding, but there was no complaint, either then or afterward, from any of them.

Only one major plan had to be changed. Mary and I were engaged to be married in June of 1959. Dad and the family booked a flight out of Canada to Africa for January 19, 1959. At that time, it was against the college rules for students to get married during the college semesters. But there was no way I was going to be married without my parents present. With trepidation, I walked into the college president's office. I didn't asked for permission, I simply announced to him that Mary and I were getting married on January 17. Rev. C.B. Smith just looked at me, then smiled and said, "Congratulations!" (I suspect he new quite well about Dad's leaving and our pre-empted plan for marriage in June.)

No complaints from me or Mary either.

There were many things to do to get ready to go to Africa: vaccinations, passports, barrels packed, tickets purchased. Some goods had to be disposed of, and someone had to have the power of attorney for Mom and Dad in their absence. The secretary-treasurer of the church agreed to do that, and faithfully looked after all of Dad's affairs for the full two years. Dad was Assistant Superintendent of the District at that time, and was also holding several other high offices.

A leave of absence was given by the church, and an interim pastor had to be found. Rev. James Peirce was agreed upon for the specific period of two years while Mom and Dad and the three juniors were in Africa. He did well. He had the use of the parsonage and Mom and Dad's furniture. The church paid Mom and Dad an amount for the use of the furniture.

Two days before they left, Dad and Rev. Willis MacPherson, Mary's pastor, performed our wedding. Two days later, we all bid them farewell at the church. On the day of their departure, it was freezing rain, blocking access to the road to the airport. They had to drive miles out of their way and arrived after departure time, but the plane's departure had also been delayed. It had to be de-iced, and they sat in it for more than an hour before take-off. Their connection in New York was also delayed, so in Paris they caught a rickety old DC-4 to Rome. They arrived there just in time for the next flight to Nairobi.

Five weeks from appointment, they were in Nairobi.

They were met there by a number of missionaries whom they knew well, and others who had preached in Dad's pulpit in Oshawa. They welcomed them warmly and arranged that they stay in the Ainsworth Hotel until they could find permanent housing.

Exactly two years from their leaving Canada, they were able to announce, "Mission Accomplished."

The Building of Nairobi Evangelistic Centre

One of the first priorities when Dick, Olive, and their three youngest children arrived in Nairobi was to search for land on which to build the "Nairobi Evangelistic Centre."

For the first while, Dick continued the meetings in the tent, until about a month after they arrived, when they were able to rent Rahimtulla Hall on Jevanji Street. The minister of housing, The Honourable Musa Amalemba, was Dick's translator on many occasions in that spacious hall.

The colonial authorities had refused to give them a grant of land in the city centre, but had suggested a property in the Lavington area, out in the suburbs and quite a distance from the city centre. Dick was not one to give up quickly!

They rented a house on the edge of town, where there was no

light in the streets, and the nights were as black as pitch. Young four-year-old Rick was afraid to get out of bed in the mornings. Dick and Olive felt "led" to get Rick a bike from their meagre funds. Rick suddenly recovered!

Dick looked at an old theatre in an acceptable place, but the cost of refurbishing it from its rundown condition would be as much as building a new structure. Dick and others, including the Field Secretary, John McBride, haunted the real estate agents, but to no avail. The answer was usually, "We'll call you if anything comes in." No calls came.

One day, Dick was doing business at the Standard Bank on Delamere Avenue, now called Kenyatta Avenue, and as he came out of the bank, he had a distinct and strong impression. He was to see an Estate Lawyer in "Mansion House" nearby. It was a very clear impression. In spite of the fact that he had been told already, "Don't call us, we'll call you..." he headed into Mansion House.

It was not easy to get by the receptionist. She insisted that he should have an appointment. After some pressure from Dick, she finally relented and went into the inner offices. After a suitable delay, she returned, stating that he could go in, but added, "But you *really* should have made an appointment," nose in the air.

When Dick went in, the lawyer also reminded Dick that he needed an appointment. He was very busy, sipping a cup of cold tea. The lawyer also reminded him, quite sharply, that Dick was not to call, but that they would call *him*! Then he went on to explain that they had nothing in their files and that they would call him if anything came up. Goodbye!

Dick was reluctant to leave. The inner voice had been so insistent that he just stood there and stared at the lawyer. I suspect Dick gave him "The Look." This needs some explanation.

All five of us, as Dick's children, knew what "The Look" was. It was used to communicate with overpowering clarity what was on

Dad's mind. "The Look" could silence you! It could motivate you. It could make you feel guilty. It could convey both questions and answers. We have all experienced it, and I suspect many others have seen that benign but powerful "Look."

Dick just stood and waited. The lawyer became a little agitated and impatient, shuffling papers on his desk. Then a surprised look came on his face. "Just a moment," he said, and he rang for the receptionist. He told her to bring in a certain file, which she did. He studied it for a few moments, and then, rather ungraciously, said, "This could be what you are looking for."

It was on a major main street, Valley Road. Almost an acre with a house on one side and a large tennis court on the other; large enough to build what they had planned. The price was within what Dick had been authorized to spend. Dick immediately wrote out a cheque to bind the deal.

He went to the post office nearby, and wired John McBride, the Field Secretary who was on vacation. The immediate response from Mombasa was, "Grab it!"

It was a leasehold property which did not expire until the end of the century (this was in 1959). The payment on the leasehold property was Kshs. 20.00 per year in lieu of taxes (about $3.00). And it was renewable at the turn of the millennium.

Dick and his family moved into the house on the property on the last day of July 1959, after more than three months of negotiating and red tape.

Dick had been given two years to find a property and build a centre for multi-racial evangelism. Exactly two years later, they arrived back in Canada with the "Mission Accomplished."

Meanwhile, during the building of the church in Nairobi, Dick held meetings in the house that came with the property on Valley Road. It was formerly the home of a Bishop of the Church of England. Thus, the leasehold arrangement.

Dick began meetings immediately in the house on the new property: Sunday services, Wednesday night Bible studies, and Saturday night prayer meetings.

A building was designed, a builder contracted, and work began.

Who Did It?

When Dick spoke in meetings with the Indian people, he always gave opportunity for the people to ask questions. There were Hindus, Muslims, Jains, Seiks, and probably people from other Eastern religions, along with Indian Christians.

A young woman raised her hand, indicating she had a question. Brother Macwan, their Indian Christian host of these meetings, interpreted her question: "Can you heal my hand?" She held up her hand, and her fingers hung as though there was no life in them.

She went on to explain that she was a manual telephone operator in a large office and her hand was becoming progressively useless. She felt she was in danger of losing her job.

The young lady sat down between Dick and Olive, and Dick reached across and asked to hold her hand. He then asked everyone to join in prayer for her healing. Following the prayer, Dick held on to her hand for a moment. He admitted later he was fearful that when he let go, nothing would have happened.

Finally he said, "Now see what you can do with your hand." At once she began to flex her fingers, hand, and elbow. There was an exclamation of surprise from those gathered. Dick then pointed at an Indian who was known as a "holy man" and almost shouted at him, "Who did that? Who did that?"

For a moment, the holy man merely stared at Dick, then, when he found his voice, he said, "Jesus Christ did it!"

Quickly, Dick turned to an elderly Muslim woman and repeated his question to her: "Who did that?" Immediately she answered with the same answer, "Jesus Christ did it!" Then Dick went from one to the other, and without hesitation or exception, they all agreed, Jesus must have done it.

Dick was careful to explain that he could not heal anyone, that only Jesus could do such things. It gave him a great opening to preach Jesus Christ to that mixed crowd.

"His Name, through faith in His Name has made this... strong."

Some Miracles Just Seem to Happen!

She was a shut-in, and Dick had been asked to visit her in her home. She was a stately woman, and tall, which was obvious even though she was sitting in a wheelchair.

During the visit, when Dick would normally chat for a while, then offer to pray for the home and family, he also encouraged the woman to come to church to be with the assembled believers in a meeting.

Not altogether surprising, she did arrive at the church the following Sunday morning in her wheelchair. Her husband and another friend carried her, in the wheelchair, up the broad steps of the church and into the sanctuary. She was "parked" about halfway up the aisle toward the front of the church.

Dick preached a Bible-centred message as was his usual habit, using it not just for his text, but gleaning illustrations for his sermon from it as well. At the close of the service, he did again what he very often did. He gave a general invitation for people to come to the front of the church for individual prayer. "Whatever you need from the Lord, come forward, and we will pray with you."

With the help of her husband, the lady slowly stood to her feet and, with a shuffling walk, each step about two inches, and holding to canes, she made her way forward. She stood right in the centre of the aisle at the front, with several others standing across the front of the altar.

It seemed the devil spoke into Dick's mind, saying, "Nothing is going to happen to her, so you had better leave her until the last!" Had Dick obeyed that impulse, he would have been in doubt as to what might have happened. So, he disobeyed doubt!

He went immediately to her and, as was his very normal approach, asked the lady what she wanted the Lord to do for her. With some show of almost indignant surprise, she said, "Why, I want to walk, of course!"

Dick laid his hands on her hands, which were grasping the tops of her canes, and simply asked the Lord to do for her what she desired. Then he asked her if she could lift her foot. She did. Then he told her to lift it higher. She did. Then he told her to lift her other foot in the same way.

She looked very pleased, and Dick went on to ask, "Do you think you can walk now?" She replied without a moment's hesitation, "Of course, I can!" She tucked her two canes under one arm, turned around, and walked in a perfectly normal way all the way to the back of the church without any assistance. Her husband and their friend watched her in amazement.

After walking around for some time, giving thanks to the Lord the whole while, she returned to a seat, leaving her wheelchair in the aisle. By this time, most of the congregation was in tearful praise to God, rejoicing with her.

"Ye Shall Be Witnesses"

Jenty's crippled leg was one and a half inches shorter than his other. He walked with a very distinctive wobble. His life took a startling change when he encountered Christians who believed that God could heal his leg. He was prayed for and his short leg, by actual clinical measurement, was lengthened by the full one and a half inches. The result was that he accepted Jesus Christ as his personal Lord and Saviour. He was "born again."

In those regular Saturday evening prayer meetings held in the Bombay home in Nairobi, people were praying particularly that God would pour out His Spirit on the Indian community. At the end of one of the Saturday prayer meetings, Jenty, who's full name was Jayentalal Shah, came to Dick with a question. "Sahib," he said, "while I was praying in my own language (Gujarati) I began to speak a language I do not know. What was that?"

Dick explained that he had been filled with the Holy Ghost, and went on to further explain that God had given him this gift to be used for God's glory. Jenty continued to go to the prayer meetings and would often be heard quietly praying in other tongues.

Several months passed, and one Sunday, Olive, who was the Sunday School Superintendent in the Nairobi Evangelistic Centre, was faced with a problem. The Gujarati lady who normally taught a class of Gujarati children was unable to come to teach her class. She had no other teacher to call into the class, so she approached Jenty. Rather diffidently, she asked if he would read the English language lesson and then translate it into Gujarati for the children.

She apologized for being unable to give him time to prepare and made reference to his lack of experience. But she did ask him to teach the class.

Jenty looked at Olive rather shyly and said, "Memsahib, I think I can do it all right. Ever since I received the Holy Ghost, I have been gathering children behind my father's greengrocer shop and have been telling these stories from the Bible. They come every Saturday, and I have quite a few."

Did not Jesus say about the Holy Spirit, "He shall testify of Me"?

Dick learned some time later that Jenty was the first recorded Hindu believer who was baptized in Kenya. He learned this from a Christian newspaper published in India.

Shortly after that, more Hindus became believers through various miracles and the faithful teaching of God's Word. And word got around!

The Southern Baptists (USA) had a church in Nairobi. One day, their American supervisor and the local missionary came to visit Dick at home. They questioned him as to how they were reaching the Hindus. They had a few nominal Christians from India, but in twelve years they had not succeeded in converting one Kenyan Hindu to Christ. Dick said, "Brethren, I don't want to try to change your theology, but it is through the power of the Holy Spirit and the preaching of the Gospel, accompanied by signs and wonders, that God has, at last, reached these people."

They rejected Dick's words and went home dejected, still determined to work without the baptism of the Holy Ghost. A little like the rich young ruler, they went away sorrowfully.

Some time later, the Thursday evening meetings were being held in the home of an Indian couple. Both the husband and wife were teachers in schools in the city of Nairobi, and both were active in the church. They gathered their neighbours who were Muslims, Hindus, and Jains, and perhaps some other religions.

When they prayed in those meetings, opportunity was given for anyone to make a special personal request for prayer, with some remarkable results.

A Muslim man asked for prayer for his wife's mother who had suffered a stroke and had been in a coma for many days in their home. All the various requests were brought before the Lord in prayer in the meeting.

When the meeting concluded, this Muslim man asked if Dick and Olive could follow him in his car to his home. Since it was on their way home in any case, they consented. The man went in to the house ahead of Dick and Olive to prepare his wife for visitors. Almost immediately, he rushed out and asked Dick and Olive to come in. The household was quite bewildered and in turmoil.

The first thing he had seen when he entered his wife's room was his mother-in-law sitting up in bed, just finishing eating. He was so startled that he forgot to tell his wife that there would be visitors and brought Dick and Olive right in. He excitedly asked his wife what had happened. She told him:

"About an hour ago, mother suddenly became conscious, sat up, and asked for food. She said she was hungry. So I prepared food and she has just finished eating."

The husband asked what time this had taken place, and when they compared the times, it was as near as could be ascertained to the time the people had been praying for her in the meeting.

She appeared to be perfectly well, and the next day, she got up from her bed as normally as before she was stricken.

"Before they call, I will answer; and while they are still speaking, I will hear" (Isaiah 65:24).

The Young "Not Quite Gentleman," Until...

Two young nurses had come out from England to work at the hospital for their support, but mainly to give witness to their faith in the Lord. They *did* have a captive audience!

They told Dick and Olive of a young man named John who had experienced a serious nervous breakdown. They asked if they could bring him to the Bombay home, which was only a short distance from the hospital. One of the nurses accompanied him, and when she had introduced him, she went out to the kitchen with Olive, leaving the young fellow with Dick.

The young fellow told Dick that he had gone to the Church of England and had been a choir boy – but that had been some years ago. He had been sent out by the Prudential Insurance Company as manager in the Kenya office, and he had prospered.

Since he was an unmarried young man in foreign surroundings, he looked for companionship and pleasure, as so many expatriates have done under similar circumstances. His life of excess and sin had caught up with him, and on top of all that, he had contracted Bilharzia, a water-born disease. It was a disease which, if left untreated, would kill anyone. He was receiving treatment for this, which, at that time, was a very rugged form of treatment.

Dick told him the simple Gospel, the only kind he knew. John was ready to listen, and when Dick knew he fully understood what he was talking about, Dick asked him a question: "Are you ready to surrender your life to Christ?" He answered that he was ready and wanted to.

Dick told him that he would pray for him first, and then the young man should pray for himself. The young fellow said he was afraid he couldn't remember any of the prayers he had learned as a boy. Dick said that he would help him.

Dick prayed first, as he said he would. After a few moments, John tried to pray a prayer of penitence which he had once learned from the Prayer Book. After several attempts, he could not remember it right and became silent. Dick had just begun to think he had given up and was about to speak out to lead him in a prayer. This was something Dick had done any number of times in leading people to repentance and faith in the Lord.

Suddenly, he heard a sob which seemed to come from deep within John. He then burst out spontaneously in the simplest terms, saying, "O God, please have mercy on me, I'm a sinner!" Then there seemed to roll out of him such a confession, not only of his sins, but of his deep longing for God, as a soul who had just found his way home.

When he ended, Dick prayed for him again, then waited to give the young man time to compose himself. Dick knew John was a very conservative British type who would be most reluctant to display any emotion.

When the nurse and Olive returned from the kitchen, John voluntarily told them what had happened to him. Great joy was felt, as they fellowshipped together. John later received the baptism in the Holy Spirit, and was also baptized in water. He became very active in the Nairobi Evangelistic Centre (now called Nairobi Pentecostal Church, and sometimes known as the "Christ is the Answer" Church).

Dick and Booze

During the Christmas season of 1960, the Bombays were invited 'up-country' to Nyang'ori to help the various churches in their Christmas Day services. These were unusual services, compared to what the family was used to in Canada. The service started when everyone got there. Starting time was not too important. What *was* important was that the meeting would go on all day. Though announced for 9:00 a.m., meetings usually began at about 10:30 or after. Choir competitions, singing, several sermons, feasting, and more singing and preaching marked Christmas Day in Kenya. This was the day the Saviour was born; "it belongs to Him."

Dad was at one church, Mom was at another, and Ruth, then seventeen, was at another. Lois and Rick accompanied either Mom or Dad.

When Christmas Day was all over, Christmas was celebrated the next day with the missionaries from Nyang'ori and Goibei, both near Kisumu on Lake Victoria. This was up in the hills among the Maragoli and Nandi tribes.

Mom and Dad's "houseboy" was left in charge of the house back in Nairobi while the family was "up-country."

When they arrived back in Nairobi, there was a box of choice groceries on the dining room table. There was a vacant spot in the box where it appeared some item had been "lifted" out. But there was plenty left for Dick to know the donor had meant well. A bottle of "Vat 90" and another of "Marshall's Gin" were among the other well chosen foods.

They could not imagine who would send such a gift, for, of course, Mom and Dad drank no alcohol in any form. As far as they knew, none of their new friends in Nairobi drank. They even asked their Indian grocer if he had sent it, but he knew nothing of it. They ended up trading the liquor at their regular grocery store for more acceptable groceries.

They finally found out who sent it.

Dick had been invited to an Indian Muslim home where an old lady lay helpless with an obvious "dropsy" condition, locally known as "dropsicle." Her arms on the bed were like sacs of water.

She was unable to speak English, and Dick had only her eleven-year-old granddaughter to act as an interpreter. Dick struggled as he tried to tell the old lady about the Saviour. She listened and nodded her head from time to time. This happened on several occasions as he explained the Gospel to her. When he thought she might at last have understood, Dick prayed for her and asked God to heal her.

When Dick visited her again, she had improved to the point where she could sit up and feed herself without any assistance.

Her son, who had first called Dick to his mother's sick bed, owned a whole string of various kinds of shops, including a grocery shop and liquor store. This Christmas gift had come from him with his best wishes and a note of gratitude for Dick's ministry to his mother.

Later, at the time of a Muslim feast, the same Indian sent Dick the "other half" of a goat which had been killed in remembrance of the ram which Abraham offered in the place of Isaac. The family ate it, but in remembrance of "the Lamb of God which takes away the sins of the world."

Dick had a remarkable ministry among the Indian people. Perhaps the name "Bombay" was some attraction, but he gained a reputation among them as a man to whom God listened and, as a result, healed people.

The Italian Connection

During the Second World War, many Italian prisoners of war were taken in Somaliland and Eritrea and held in prisoner of war camps in Kenya. They built a beautiful little chapel on the highway down the escarpment from the Nairobi highlands into the Great Rift Valley. Many, when they were released after the war, had found Kenya a pleasant place and returned. Some of them took up farming.

The son of one of these farmers, Walter, had become a mechanic in Nairobi. He had been saved and attended the Centre on Valley Road. He was disowned by his family because of his abandonment of their traditional denomination. As a result, Walter was at Dick's home often, in addition to attending the church consistently. He was eventually transferred to Kampala, Uganda, where he was of great assistance to the missionaries there. Dick saw him only once after his transfer.

Walter told Dick and Olive that his father had a very serious case of asthma, and that he had urged his father to go to the Centre to be prayed for. Walter had seen many miraculous healings.

One day, the father appeared in a meeting, although Dick did not know who he was at the time. When the time came for people to be prayed for, this man stepped forward. Every breath was a struggle. His face was flushed, and he dripped with perspiration.

As Dick usually did, he asked, "What would you like the Lord to do for you?" All Dick got was a blank stare as the man continued to struggle for breath. After Dick tried several times to get an answer, he realized the man spoke no English. Someone told Dick he was Italian. He probably knew Swahili, but Dick did not speak Swahili, and there was no one present who could interpret.

Suddenly, Dick remembered that when he had pastored in North Bay, years before, a large proportion of his congregation was Italian. Some of the young people had taken it upon themselves to teach Dick Italian. He had learned quite a bit, but after all these years, he had forgotten it.

Yet, as he stood facing the man, there flashed into Dick's mind a verse he had memorized in Italian. He didn't know if he could say it well, or even if the dialect he had learned would fit this man's understanding. Should he try it?

"Ile salario de peccato e morte, ma ile donna de Deo e vita eterna per Jesu Christo nosto Signore" came out stumblingly. The man looked blank. Dick felt urged to try it again. This time when Dick opened his mouth, the words flowed easily and clearly. Recognition showed in his face. Dick kept repeating it, over and over again, and the man began to nod his head vigourously. Then he said, *"Si, si, Signor!"*

Dick gave the "Word" time to work on the man, and then he prayed for him.

When Dick opened his eyes, the man was breathing normally, his flush diminished. The man mopped the sweat from his face, took several deep breaths, and smiled some more.

Walter's father had found Jesus, the Healer.

For the wages of sin is death, but the gift of God is eternal life in Jesus Christ our Lord (Romans 6:23).

True in any language!

24

Outside Nairobi

An Angel's Foot

Dick was often in demand as a conference speaker, not just in North America, but also in Africa. He and Ernie Francis, another Canadian missionary, were invited to speak at what turned out to be the last Assemblies of God conference in the Congo (Zaire). They, along with their wives, would have to drive to Andudu where the Missions Headquarters was located in the Congo. It would turn into a most interesting trip by car.

On the trip, Dick asked Ernie if he ever felt reluctant about preaching what the Lord had laid on his heart. Ernie could not recall such an experience. Dick told Ernie that he felt that way about what had been laid on his heart by the Lord, but did not tell Ernie what the message was.

Arrangements had been made to make an overnight stay at an

Africa Inland Mission Station at the foot of the Ruwenzori Mountains, better known perhaps as the Mountains of the Moon. Dick was driving, and as he turned off the main road to negotiate the narrow winding road to the foothills, the elephant grass slapped the car on both sides. The road was just two ruts with weeds and grass between. Sight was limited by the height of the grass and the curves in the road.

Rounding a curve, they saw a body lying across the road. Instinct and many years of driving experience caused Dick to lift his foot from the gas to put it on the brakes – but suddenly his foot slammed down on the gas pedal. Quicker than thought, he geared down into a lower gear and blew the car horn loudly and long. The body on the road quickly came to life, leaping into the tall grass. As they rounded the next short curve, four or five men, armed with clubs, were ranged across the road. The noise of the engine and the sound of the horn warned them that they would be run down if they stayed. They leaped for the sides of the road, and the car whipped past them. They had no knowledge of how dangerous it had become in the Congo just before independence, though they had heard of some atrocities.

When they arrived at the A.I.M. Station and told the missionaries of their experience, they were horrified. Just the week before, a car had been waylaid on the same road, and neither the car nor the people had been seen again.

Dick always contended that an angel must have stepped on his toe as he tried to raise it from the gas pedal. How else to explain it?

As they continued their journey the next day, they were more cautious and alert.

Dick was to be the speaker at the opening meeting. He read from 1 Peter 5:1-9:

...you younger people, submit yourselves to your elders. Yes, all of you be submissive to one another, and be clothed with humility.

As Dick began to preach, he noticed that his interpreter, a missionary, was having difficulty speaking. Looking back at his notes, Dick saw that the last thing he had said was, "I have gone to conferences to promote certain things, but was overruled by the brethren. I submitted and went home with more joy, peace, and blessing than had I gained my own point."

By this time, Dick's interpreter was is real trouble. He looked deathly pale and was hardly able to continue. Dick stopped and, seeing his condition, asked if he would like another interpreter to replace him. He declined and asked for a glass of water. Dick continued along the same line of submission – the younger to the older – all, to the will of the church and each other. The interpreter was having a hard time, but continued to the end.

Dick and Ernie and their wives were to stay in the home of the Superintendent. As they were having cool drinks before they went to bed, the Superintendent asked Dick if he knew anything of the difficulties they were having with one of their associates. Dick knew nothing. He had never met any of them before and had not heard anything about it.

The Superintendent said that Dick had described their situation as accurately as though he had been told the whole thing. He went on to tell how Dick's interpreter had determined on a course of action which would take him to a place of extreme danger. Since this was only weeks before the Congo achieved independence, there had been a lot of killing of Europeans (white people from anywhere). This was particularly true in that specific area.

Dick's interpreter insisted that God had told him to go, and when the conference was over, he went – against the advice of his elders in missionary ministry. When the conference was over, Dick and company returned to Nairobi. The rest is history – awful history.

The interpreter and his wife were taken hostage by a political faction called "The Lion Men." His wife was eventually released, but the young missionary was brutally beaten to death, and his body was thrown to the crocodiles.

In Africa, rain can affect almost anything you do. A tropical downpour can hardly be described in North American terms. During the rainy season, you can almost set your watch to a downpour at about 2:30 p.m. every day in the Kisii area of Kenya.

Dick had been invited by Paul Hawkes, resident missionary at that time among the Kisii people, to preach a series of meetings. Problem. The thatch roof of the church had become so sodden in the past several rainy seasons that, this year, it finally collapsed. There was no church in which to hold the meetings. The Christians were disappointed and the non-Christians were laughing and joking about the whole matter.

However, a crowd had gathered, and they went ahead with the meetings outdoors, both morning and afternoon. On the first day, heavy rain clouds formed, and the unbelievers watched and waited for the service to be rained out; 2:30 p.m. came and went – and the rain held off. At the conclusion of the afternoon service, when they had packed up their equipment and gotten into the car, the rain came – in torrents.

This happened every day. At the conclusion of the afternoon service, after packing the car and getting in, the rains would come. Every day. This did as much to convince the unbelievers as the preaching, and many came to accept Jesus Christ as Saviour.

Rain was predicted to affect meetings where Dick was to preach at a place called Virembe, in Western Kenya. It was said that, because it was the beginning of the rains, everyone would still be planting and no one would be willing to come to the meetings. There had been drought for several growing seasons. However, the people were encouraged to come, believing that God would send the rains at the right time.

Many people were saved and filled with the Spirit. Many

confessed that they had not tithed for a long time. Dick was asked to do some teaching on tithing. The next day, people brought eggs, fruit, chickens, and vegetables. Many miracles took place, and the blessing of God was on those meetings.

While driving to the meeting one day, a small boy ran alongside the car, asking them to stop and come pray for a paralyzed man.

The man, who had been a believer, had become rich through his brick-making business – but had forgotten the Lord. He was prayed for, for both forgiveness and healing, since he had become a cripple as well. Later the same day, he gave this testimony:

"The pastor and the missionary prayed for me this morning. I have been a cripple for many years. When I called on Jesus to save me and heal me, I felt a warmth all through my body, and strength came to my legs and hands. I got up from where I was and went into my house to tell my family. Then I got dressed and came up here to the church. I feel like a young man again. I feel like I want to run!"

Dick, through the interpreter, told him to go ahead and run. He ran down the aisle, out the door, and round and round the church. Every time he passed a door or window, the people would raise a great shout.

He was still running after the service was over and when Dick and the others left.

Some years later, when Dick was back in Canada and my wife, Mary, and I were living at a place called Nyang'ori, we heard of one of the multiple miracles which had taken place.

It is considered a shameful thing in Africa for a wife not to be able to bear children. In one meeting, Dick prayed for a goodly number of women who were barren. Within the next year, most of them had baby boys, some of them had girls. Most of them were named "Bombay" in honour of the man who had prayed for their mothers. This was at either Virembe or Jemovo, in Western Kenya.

When Dick was preaching a series of meetings at Jemovo, many people were saved, filled with the Spirit, and healed.

One morning, Arn Bowler, who had been a member of Dick's church in Oshawa and was now a missionary in Kenya, brought a young woman to Dick. Arn asked Dick, "Do you recognize her?"

She had been prayed for the previous day. She was the daughter of one of the pastors and, for eleven years, had been ill, covered with running sores. Because of the stench, she lay in a hut by herself, unable to move about. She would swell up to such a degree, at times, that her skin would split. She was in constant pain.

People had carried her in to Dick for prayer, and carried her back out, unchanged. But some time during the night, she was made perfectly whole. She got up in the morning and dressed herself. She picked up a five-gallon water container, went down Jemovo hill to the stream, and brought back the full five gallons balanced on her head in the African fashion.

Now, here she stood before Dick, perfectly whole. Thirteen years later, Dick was in Kenya on his way home from Thailand with Olive, and they went "up-country" not too far from Jemovo. He enquired about the young lady. She was married, had children, and lived quite a normal life.

At that same meeting, a young boy who had a severely crippled foot and walked on his ankle with the foot turned in was healed – partially at first. His foot straightened out, but the next day, his one leg was still crooked; bowed.

The next day, Dick saw him and asked him to come forward. The boy did. Dick asked, "Wouldn't you like to run and play football with the other boys?"

He answered, "*Ndio Bwana*" (Yes, Sir).

Dick put his hand on the boy's head and simply prayed, "Lord, do for this boy what he wants You to do."

Dick turned him around, patted him on the behind. and sent

him to his seat. He had only taken two or three steps when, suddenly, the crooked leg snapped back and became straight right before their eyes.

The boy turned with a wide grin and said, *"Asante sana, Bwana!"* (Thank you very much, Sir!)

There was a great shout to the Lord. Who wouldn't?

25

A Most Outstanding Influence

While Dick and Olive were in Kenya, the Mau Mau movement, which began in 1951, had just concluded, but rigid controls were still in place. Pressure was being put on the Colonial Government for Kenya to attain its independence. Some of the colonial police force were often over-zealous in their attempts at keeping the peace. A great deal of tension filled the country.

Although the world press reported on the slaughter of white settlers and some of the horrors that accompanied that, the fact remains that many thousands more Africans were killed compared to the relatively few white people. It was a time of fear, hate, recrimination, revenge, and violent action and reaction.

One day, Dick and Olive were having lunch, listening to the one hour of radio available. It was the news. As they listened to the news, they were shocked to hear that a white man had shot and killed an African "house boy." He was arrested immediately, charged with first degree murder, and would face trial. It had happened very near to where they lived.

In their regular Saturday evening prayer meeting, two British Christians who attended began to anguish in prayer for the salvation of this young twenty-nine-year-old. As they prayed, they groaned and cried out to God rather loudly. The following Saturday night in the prayer meeting, one of the prison guards attended and asked Dick to visit young Peter Richard Poole in the prison.

Although it was extremely difficult to make such a visit, the prison guard phoned the following day stating that he had obtained permission for Dick to visit. But when he arrived for the visit, he was turned down, since he did not represent the church to which Peter Poole had a traditional connection. Dick persisted. Finally, he was allowed to visit Peter once in the "Common Room" where Peter was chained to two white guards.

On Dick's first visit with Peter Poole, he learned a few things about Peter and the murder. He worked as an electrician in a shop his father owned. He had gone home for lunch and then lay down for a short rest. He heard his two German Shepherd dogs barking fiercely. He jumped up, grabbed his Luger pistol, and went outside to see what was going on.

The dogs were lunging and barking at an African going by on a bicycle. The Kenyan picked up a stone to try to fend off the dogs, frantically trying to get away. Peter thought the African was teasing his dogs. In a rage, he fired his Luger, knocking the Kenyan to the ground. He then fired another shot which killed the man instantly. This part of the story was never ever brought up again in the conversations between Dick and Peter.

Peter was a wild man. He threw food in the faces of his guards, cursed them, and fought with them. He had killed other Africans in the Aberdares where anyone sited was assumed to be a Mau Mau "freedom fighter."

Because it was so distracting with other prisoners around, Dick was finally allowed to visit Peter the second time in his cell, through the good graces of the prison superintendent, who happened to be from Saskatoon in Canada. He was Irish in background. This provided a useful "Canadian Connection."

Always, Peter was chained to two prison guards for these visits. Dick visited him every week, during which time Peter went through his court case and was condemned to death by hanging.

This was the first time in the history of the Colony that a white man had been condemned to death for killing a black man.

Peter had seldom attended his own church. Dick read the Scriptures to him, sitting across a small table from Peter. Dick prayed with him. He took a New Testament to him, read, and underlined certain verses for Peter to read and consider. The soldiers who were manacled to Peter would lean down to see the Scriptures Dick was explaining. After a time, as God's plan of salvation was explained to Peter, his heart began to open, and one day, he invited Jesus Christ into his life.

Dick explained to the prison Superintendent that Peter wanted to be baptized, and Dick always baptized by immersion. How could they do that? A few days later, the Superintendent told Dick that they had made an arrangement. A large six-foot-long bathtub had been set up in the prison yard, one leg missing, but propped up with bricks.

There was tight security, with prison guards all around. Peter's mother and father had come out from England to visit and be near their son. With prisoners, black, white, and brown, looking through the bars all around the prison yard, Dick baptized Peter in the bathtub. They then went into the prison where Dick served communion to Peter and his parents together.

Appeals were made, first to the Governor of the Colony of Kenya, then to the Privy Council in the UK, and eventually to the Queen. All were rejected. After these rejections had been noted, a date was set for Peter to be hanged until dead. At that point, Dick began to visit Peter every day.

The prison Superintendent asked Dick at one point, "What have you done to this young man? When he came in here he was a wild man! Now he's as meek as a lamb!" Dick answered, "That's what the Gospel does. I didn't do it! The Gospel changes people, not I."

Two days before Peter was to be hanged, he told Dick, "I have some very bitter thoughts in my heart against some people, including my lawyer who let me down. If I'm going to die the day after tomorrow, I don't want to die with this bitterness in me!"

Dick breathed a quick prayer, and John 15:7 came to his mind. He took Peter's New Testament and read it to him: "If you abide in Me, and My words abide in you, you will ask what you desire, and it shall be done for you." Dick then added, "If you ask the Lord to 'do for you' what is necessary to rid you of that bitterness, God will do it." Dick had to leave almost immediately.

When he came back the next day, he spent time with Peter. When he was about to leave, Peter looked at Dick with a little smile and said, "It works!" Dick was a bit puzzled, having forgotten yesterday's conversation, and asked, "What works?" Peter had memorized the Scripture and quoted it back to Dick, saying, "He's done it to me; God has removed all the bitterness!" He added, "I can go to meet God with a clean heart and a clear conscience." Peter had a bright and shining testimony both to the other prisoners, but particularly to the guards, who knew the kind of man he had been, not just as a prisoner, but as a soldier fighting the Mau Mau.

God knew all that, cleansed Peter's heart, and made a new man out of him. Dick left that day, promising to spend the whole of the next day with him, since they were to execute him at 8:00 p.m. Dick returned early in the morning, spent the whole day with Peter, having a little lunch with the prison chaplain who had just returned from his leave. Dick was glad for that, since attending an execution was one of the things he had never ever wanted to do. "I never wanted to minister to a person who was about to be executed. I'm just as human as anyone else, and maybe more so."

The prison doctor and the Superintendent came three times to Peter's cell, and in Dick's presence, Peter turned down the sedative which was offered and which would have made him oblivious to what was happening. Peter simply thanked them and said, "No, I don't need anything."

Meanwhile, outside the prison, a large crowd had gathered. Kenyans had come to see that justice was done, and many Asians and Whites had come, hoping somehow to intervene. There were armed soldiers standing at six-foot intervals, with rifles ready, to control the crowd.

An hour before the execution, the doctor and Superintendent once more came to offer a sedative, but Peter again said, "No, thank you. I am ready to go." They then moved him to the room adjacent to the execution room. Once again, Dick served communion, with the Anglican Chaplain, the doctor, and the prison Superintendent. A doctor had to be present at every execution.

After the communion, the Anglican priest said, "Brother Bombay, I've never been in a communion service like that in my life! Jesus was right there with us!"

A gong sounded, and everyone had been instructed as to what they must do. They walked up the long ramp to the execution chamber. The hangman quickly threw a heavy strap around Peter, pinning his arms to his sides, then drew a black hood over his head. Dick and the Anglican priest were each told to walk beside Peter, holding his head gently and talking to him. They chose to repeat the twenty-third psalm, and Peter joined them in repeating it over and over again. Suddenly, the door was flung open and four British officers picked Peter up and stood him on painted footprints on the trap door.

Very quickly the trap was sprung, and Peter died. Dick said, "You have no idea how I felt in that situation." Dick turned to look at the others, and the four officers were standing in the corners weeping and sobbing like children. They knew Peter was ready to go because Peter had witnessed to them, testifying about his new life in Jesus Christ. Even the hangman stood off to one side in amazement at the peace Peter had exhibited. The presence of the Lord seemed to move right into that execution chamber.

The law required that the body must hang for an hour to assure death. During that hour, Dick and the others went home to where Olive had prepared tea. Dick's hand shook and the cup rattled in his hand as he tried to come to grips with the reality of what he had just witnessed.

When an hour had passed, they went back for the burial outside the prison. Large search lights had been set up outside where the soldiers were watching the gathered throng of people. They had feared riots, since this was the first execution of a white man in the whole history of Kenya.

Peter's body had been put in a box and placed on a cart. Followed by several vehicles, they made their way to the hill side graveyard where a grave had already been dug. A simple kerosene lamp provided the only light for the burial. Dick had to commit the body to the grave.

Dick said, "I shall never forget the sense, the feeling I had, when I said, 'As it hath pleased Almighty God to take unto Himself the spirit of our brother here departed in hope, certain sure hope, of the resurrection through Jesus Christ our Lord, we therefore commit his body to the ground in the Name of the Father, and of the Son, and of the Holy Ghost.'"

He said later with deep emotion, "I never felt more certain than that dark night at a graveside of the certainty of the resurrection, even though I have conducted hundreds of funerals during my ministry."

That situation was the catalyst which caused a complete overhaul of the prison system in Kenya, with the introduction of evangelical pastors as chaplains, along with others who had done it exclusively for years. Through the newspapers and the radio, the whole of Kenya had been kept current on Peter Poole's trial, conviction, and execution.

Some years later, a Kenyan official of the Ministry of Education visited Dick in Canada, asking him to write up the story of Peter Poole which was included in the official history of the development of Kenya as an independent nation. Dick said, "God uses all sorts of situations and people to accomplish His will. We just have to obey. Even the weakest of us can be used by God." Dick always considered himself one of the weakest.

Every Christmas, for many years following that day, Dick and Olive received a Christmas card filled with words of gratitude from Peter Poole's parents in England.

Still the Mighty Hunter

While Dick was in Kenya building the Nairobi Evangelistic Centre on Valley Road, he went hunting game only once. The Bible School needed meat and, since Africans were not permitted to carry arms at the time because of the Mau Mau troubles, the missionaries went after the needed meat. Dick was asked to come along. This was thrilling for him, since he had enjoyed hunting in the autumn in Canada with a group of fellow ministers.

As is usual with hunters all over the world, there was considerable teasing and boasting about personal abilities to shoot well. The teasing reached a crescendo when someone missed what appeared to the others to be an easy shot.

On this hunt, two of the missionaries had missed standing shots. Amidst jibes and laughter, such excuses as, "The animals moved just as I pulled the trigger" were given. Or, "Someone spoke and spoiled my aim." That one is used in golf, too. One of them said, "A fly came and sat on my gun sight." That one could have happened, since flies abound throughout Africa. But....

These were "after-the-fact excuses," but there was the usual "before-the-fact boasts," as well. So Dick said, "I guess the old man will have to show you how!" This was met with some derision of course, as they emphasized, "Wait and see. You'll find that impala are hard to hit."

They continued to go after the herd, and after some time, were able to get ahead of them. The gun was handed to Dick, with the comment, "Here, let's see what you can do."

The impala were running past them at that point, about ninety yards away (by actual measurement later). The does were ahead, with the few bucks following, giving their warning bark as they ran and leaped. At one point, they all leaped over some hidden obstruction, so Dick aimed for the high spot of the leap. He had been warned, "You can't hit them while they are running. It's like trying to hit a flying bird with a single bullet." In spite of the fact that Dick had seen an impala leap over a twenty-foot hedge, he insisted that, "If I get the bullet there at the same time as the beast, something has got to happen."

Dick waited until he saw a pair of horns rising in the leap, then he pulled the trigger. To everyone's surprise, including Dick's, the impala went back down into the tall grass, but did not continue its next stride. It simply disappeared. When they got to where it had gone down, they found it, shot through the spine just behind the shoulder. It was dispatched quickly and neatly with a small arm.

Dick was pretty excited and well pleased, but, as befitted his age, he said calmly, "There, that is how we do it in Canada!"

The Africans were amazed, and even the missionaries were suitably impressed.

Years later, when he stopped in Kenya for a short time on his way home from Thailand, I took Dad on a hunt. When I shot an eland at 325 yards, with nothing but a peep-sight on my rifle, Dick said, "I taught you everything you know!" But Dad did pace that one out twice to make sure he could believe his eyes.

Dick admits to being only a fair shot, and quite readily says that impala shot was the luckiest he every made. He doubts he could ever have duplicated it, and, as he has often said, he was smart enough to quit while he was ahead!

He brought that impala hide home to Canada to prove... to prove what?

However, sufficient game was taken that day to last the Bible School for a good while. Isn't that why God made all those animals? (Deuteronomy 14:4-7).

Chopping With a Dull Axe

One day as Dick was walking down the street in Nairobi, he met a fellow minister, an East Indian by the name of Easu Charan. They had known each other for some time. Easu Charan looked discouraged and downcast. As they chatted, it became apparent what was bothering Dick's Indian friend.

Easu Charan had been working in the Indian community for quite a while and had never won a single soul to Christ. He was despondent. He asked Dick, "Why? Why, after all this time and work, have I never led anyone to Jesus Christ? What's wrong?"

Dick, in his rather oblique manner, said, "I think perhaps you are chopping with a dull axe." That needed some explanation, and Easu Charan asked what he meant.

Dick launched into one of his proverbial explanations. He told Easu Charan about one of his employees who, among other things, cut wood for the fireplace. He was having a tough time because his *panga* (machete) was dull. He told how he had taken the panga, and with a file, had sharpened it to a keen edge. A big grin appeared on the face of his employee when the chips flew with this new cutting edge. It wasn't long before he had a good pile of wood ready for the fireplace.

Easu Charan knew that Dick was telling him that he needed something more than theory and theology to get men saved. Then Dick told him plainly that he should ask God to baptize him in the Holy Spirit. "That will sharpen your axe!"

Easu Charan left Dick a little bit dejected and provoked. That just didn't fit into his theology. He had been taught that he had got it all when he had accepted the Lord Jesus and was sprinkled with water as a Christian.

A little later, Easu Charan met a fellow missionary and reported what Dick had told him, but without mentioning the illustration about the dull axe. The missionary told Easu Charan that perhaps Dick Bombay was right. This only added to Easu Charan's discomfort. Some time later, Easu Charan met with one of the Indian deacons and told him what Dick had said. This deacon also agreed with Dick's recommendation, which only added further to Easu Charan's unease.

Several weeks later on a Saturday evening, Easu Charan came to the regular prayer meeting in Dick's home on Valley Road. When Easu Charan greeted the people in the prayer meeting, Dick knew something had happened. Without preamble, Easu Charan asked if he could say something. Dick consented without delay, and this is what Easu Charan said:

"When Brother Bombay told me I was chopping wood with a dull axe, I was angry. When others agreed, I was angrier still. Yet I knew I must have something so that I could win men to Christ.

"That night, after I had said my prayers, I got into bed and lay awake for some time. In the darkness I heard a Voice asking, 'Easu Charan, do you love Me?' It was so real. I was not dreaming. I knew it was my Lord. I replied, 'Lord, I have served You for twenty-seven years, but I have never loved You.' I got on my knees beside my bed, and I confessed, and I wept, and I prayed all night. That morning, at four o'clock, He came to me and filled me with the Holy Ghost.

"The next day, I went to Kampala to meet with the church people. I told them what the Lord had done for me. They began to weep and dropped to their knees, asking me to pray that God would do the same thing for them. In the following two weeks, I have led more people to Jesus Christ than in all my life before."

After some time of witnessing to the Indian people, Easu Charan's denomination was greatly displeased with his having embraced the Pentecostal teaching, and they dismissed him. He went back to India where his family lived. Several months later, Dick received a letter from him. This is what some of it said:

"Since coming home, I visited my old university and had an opportunity to speak to the faculty and others. I just told them what the Lord has done for me, and they began to weep and to pray, and I led them to the Lord. Also, I spoke to the hospital staff, and the same thing happened. I am so happy. I am going all over my country to start Pentecostal meetings."

It is not highly recommended that you cut wood with a dull axe!

Mistaken Identity

Many years later, Rev. C.M. Ward, a Canadian who became the radio voice of the Assemblies of God in the U.S.A., was invited to speak at a men's conference in Ontario. Dick was unable to be present at the opening of the meeting, but went in to the meeting just as

C.M. Ward was being introduced. Dick and C.M. Ward had known each other since they were young, so when Ward saw Dick come into the meeting, he invited him to the platform. He said he had a story to tell about Dick. C.M. Ward was famous for his "stories."

This particular story had been told to C.M. Ward by a Rev. Jimmy Hooten, a Southern Baptist minister and former missionary in Africa. This is how C.M. Ward told it, with most of his facts right, quoting from Jimmy Hooten:

"I was travelling with Bombay to the northern territories of Kenya (it was actually Uganda). The country was extremely dry, and crops and cattle were in desperate need of rain. The people were gathered for a "rain dance" led by the medicine man. (In fact, it was entirely women and girls.) This was happening on the dusty road into Moroto – with no results.

"Bombay got out of the car and asked what it was all about (through an interpreter). When told, he said that only the true God could send rain. The women then demanded that Bombay pray to the true God for rain. I (Jimmy Hooten) remained in the car fearing we would be mobbed. But Bombay prayed, through the interpreter, that God would send the rain they needed so badly. There was no immediate answer, and Bombay came back into the car, and we drove away.

"We returned two days (actually four hours) later and were amazed to see the ground wet, with green beginning to show in the soil. While Bombay and I were in Moroto, clouds had formed in the area back on the road where we had come through, and a heavy rain had fallen."

There is a great deal more to the story, but then C.M. Ward turned to Dick and asked if he would confirm the story. Dick replied, "Yes, I know the story to be true, but it was not *this* Bombay who was there, but my son, who is called Calvin *Richard* Bombay."

Dick then relieved the tension caused by the mistaken identity by standing and telling a "mistaken identity" story of his own. "Two friends met who had not seen each other for a few years. The first man said, 'Congratulations, George, I hear you've made a million in oil in Texas.' The second man replied, 'Well, it was not in Texas, it was Oklahoma. It was not oil, but wheat. And it wasn't made, but lost. And it wasn't me, it was my brother!'"

The story of the rain is true. It opened the door for missionary work, and churches were planted in that area.

26

Thailand

God Leads – Dick Follows

Dick retired several times, but it never seemed to take root. It was just not in his nature to lay back and hope someone else would "do it."

A need arose on the mission field in Thailand. At a Field Fellowship Meeting, it was decided that some of the work load in bookkeeping should be spread out for several missionaries to handle. The work was divided accordingly.

It wasn't long before a problem arose. The one missionary who kept all the financial books for the field was accused, in letters to the Missions Department in Canada, of serious mismanagement of the funds and of giving unauthorized gifts to favoured national workers. Several letters were written, and it became a matter of deep concern for the International Headquarters in Toronto.

So much for retirement! Dick was the man.

In October of 1973, Dick and Olive were sent to Thailand to become senior field authority, charged with looking into the financial matters and perhaps re-organizing the whole administration of the Thailand missionary operation. What he said would be done. Olive also helped at Sharon Centre in Bangkok.

Upon arrival on November 5, they stayed with Don and Dorothy Raymer for several days until their own apartment was ready. Dick and Olive became surrogate grandparents to Rassami, the adopted Thai daughter of the Raymers. They then moved into an apartment on Soi 6 (Street 6) which they had to furnish. Their first weekend in Thailand was celebrated with "Bangkok Belly," which everyone eventually gets.

It wasn't long before Dick met with and spent time with each of the missionaries, as well as with national leaders. Meanwhile, Olive began teaching English classes for Thai women, eventually bringing some into faith in Jesus Christ. The Bible was the textbook.

The missionary who had full charge of the books never raised his voice to defend himself in the face of the accusations. In fact, he was not even aware of that being the reason Dick came to Thailand. Eventually, the matter was brought up.

Dick, together with the accused missionary, sat down with the open books for a full week, in a place away from Bangkok. After that week, the discrepancy was determined to be about two cents. Dick said to the accuser, if you are looking for something wrong with this missionary, you won't find it in here, as he held the financial records. Everything was found to be in order. When this was shared with the Field Fellowship, the missionary making the accusations was shocked. But is was simply because he himself did not understand the bookkeeping system.

There was a meeting of all the men on the field. When a specific financial "hand-out" was mentioned, where money had been given to Pastor Nirut, the books showed that indeed, money had been given. What apparently had not be known by the accuser was that this was to jointly help finance a seminar, and it had been perfectly legitimate. Dick took it upon himself to teach the accuser how to keep the books and understand them.

Dick apologized to the missionary who had been accused, on behalf of the accusing missionary. Then he commended the accused for "keeping his cool" while the accusations were flying. He then said to the missionary, "You must have felt terrible when you were accused like that!" The missionary answered, "I knew he had no grounds, so why defend myself?" Dick looked him in the eye and said, "Someday you'll make a good Superintendent!"

That missionary's wife wrote later in her diary: "He's been feeling whipped recently because of all these accusations, but he came home that day feeling 'on top.'"

Meanwhile, Olive continued teaching English, helping at the Sharon Centre, and studying Thai, together with Pastor and Mrs. Anderson of the Christian and Missionary Alliance with whom they became close friends. Dick gave a weekly Bible study for the missionaries, and one of them wrote, "We appreciate the Bombays more than words can say. Brother Bombay is a lot of fun when we get together for games occasionally in the evening, when he 'lets his hair down.' He's just what we needed!"

Scrabble™ was one of the Bombay's favourite games. Dick would usually tell stories as he tried to figure out the highest scoring word. Olive often said to him, "Cut out the preamble and play!"

While in Thailand, Dick had what he called an "eat or be eaten experience, almost...."

He went with another missionary, Carl Young, to teach at the Finnish Bible School, just outside Bangkok. Dick had taught his session and was sitting at the back of the tent while Carl led his session. Since Dick knew only a few rudimentary words in the Thai language and had used an interpreter for his session, his attention tended to wander from the matters at hand.

A slight commotion outside the tent was enough to draw his gaze in that direction. Two young men were acting strangely. One was on each side of a hedge, throwing stones as they made their way along the hedge which led right toward the tent. They picked up their pace and began to run as they continued to throw stones into the hedge.

Suddenly one of the young men yelled, "Cobra," at the same time Dick saw an eight-foot long snake darting down the hedge. Dick had no unnatural fear of snakes, but, on the other hand, he didn't feel it was the right day to try to be a hero. He leaped up onto the bench he had been sitting on and signalled others around him to do the same. They did!

A flash glimpse of a snake is not enough to determine whether a cobra is the "spitting" or "striking" variety, and Dick, not being a herpetologist, wasn't about to take up a detailed study at that moment. He knew at least that both spitting and striking cobras have a deadly venom. This knowledge alone elevated him and the others up onto the benches.

One of the young chaps who had been chasing the snake suddenly grabbed it by the tail, swung it around his head, whipping up the speed, and then whomped it onto the roadway. While it was still stunned, someone else crushed its head, and immediately the excitement was over. The teaching session continued as though nothing had happened.

Both Dick and Carl were staying at the Bible School to teach all week. They were served their meals with the students. The next day, after the classes, the cooks were kind enough to mention that today they would be eating yesterday's "catch." They were also kind enough to have cooked an alternative meal for the missionaries, just in case....

Since the snake had been a full eight feet long, it provided slices two-and-a-half inches in diameter. And, as it turned out, it was not a cobra after all, but a relatively harmless variety which had simply been out looking for its own dinner.

These "bonus" meals were not too unusual in Thailand. When there was a combination of high tides and the rainy season, the streets in Bangkok were often flooded knee deep. People waded wherever they went, whether to church or shopping. It was not uncommon to see snakes swimming down the streets, and occasionally a big fish would be trapped in shallow water. These were avidly chased by the Thais who caught them with their hands.

There's more than one way to turn a problem into a blessing!

Homeward Bound

On their way home to Canada from Thailand, Mom and Dad came to Kenya where Mary and I, with our children, were missionaries. We had wonderful fellowship. Dad did some teaching in the Bible College at Nyang'ori, and of course was invited to preach at the church he had established on Valley Road in Nairobi. It was on the same six-month trip through Kenya that I took him hunting with me and shot the eland, "just as he had taught me." Unfortunately, I could not let Dad shoot, since new hunting laws were in effect and I had a licence. A tourist's hunting licence would have cost an arm and a leg. Instead, we ate "leg of Thompson's gazelle."

Dick's daughter, Ruth, with her husband, Calvin Ratz, met them at the airport in Toronto on their return from Thailand via Kenya. The first thing Ruth said was, "Dad, there's a message at the house. You are to call right away." It turned out to be Don Cantalon, pastor in Kingston, Ontario, at the time. Don had told Ruth, "Tell him not to talk to anyone else until he talks with me!" Dick did not know him very well personally, since his only real contact with him was as a member of Don's "Canada For Christ" committee, of which Don had been an evangelist.

He explained how this had all come about. Don was losing his young assistant and was casting about, looking for the Lord's will as to who should replace him. Don had not thought of an older man, but as he drove by the District Office where Dick used to preside, he asked if anyone knew where Dick was. Don was told that Dick and Olive would be arriving that very day from overseas, and that the National Office would probably be able to tell where Don could find him. When Don arrived in Toronto, he phoned through to Ruth.

There had already been two or three invitations to consider, but Dick had given very little thought to them. But when he talked to Don Cantalon, something inside whispered, "This is it!"

Don had nothing concrete yet to offer, but asked Dick not to commit himself to anything else for a few days until Don was able to get back to Kingston. The same day another invitation came, but Dick felt no response to it.

Dick was not aware at the time that Don's assistant was gone and that he was actually looking for someone to help him. But as Dick turned from the telephone, he said to Olive, "I think this may be what the Lord has for us."

Later, Don Cantalon asked if Dick would spend a Sunday in Kingston preaching, and at that time, he may have something concrete to talk about. As it worked out, the official board of the church asked Dick to come as assistant to Don. Dick agreed.

Their more than two years in Kingston were among the most happy years of their entire ministry.

Dick tried to retire from pastoring several times! First, from pastoral work to become District Superintendent. When he retired from the District leadership, he ended up in Thailand and then Africa. When he retired from that missionary appointment, he ended up in Kingston as assistant pastor. Finally, when he retired from Kingston, he moved to Oshawa, where retirement had still not completely taken root. He preached well into his eighty-second year, with the same deep wisdom, and his preaching was in great demand.

But, as Dick quotes, "All the way, my Saviour leads me."

Kingston

Dorothy Evans was a permanent patient in St. Mary's-by-the-Lake hospital in Kingston. She had been there for many years following a brain tumour operation which had left her both blind and immobile. Pastor Don Cantalon had assigned Pastor Bombay, as the pastor of visitation, to spend as much time as possible with shut-ins and hospital patients.

It became apparent to Pastor Bombay that Dorothy was a believing Christian but had very little knowledge of Christ and many others things common to most of us. Each time he visited Dorothy, he would read a portion of Scripture to her, explaining what it meant. During those times, she would reach out and ask Dick to let her hold his hand as he read to her. One day, she asked him to describe himself to her. Did you ever try to describe yourself to someone, especially to a blind person? Dick did the best he could.

On one visit, Dick felt led to read from Revelation 21 about the "new heaven and new earth." When he had finished, Dorothy asked if there was more about heaven. He said there was, and continued to read from chapter 22. As he read, he heard Dorothy exclaim from time to time, "Oh, that's beautiful!"

On the next visit, Pastor Bombay read another portion of Scripture to her and was about to pray as he usually did, when Dorothy interrupted. She said, "Please, read again about heaven." He did, and after reading it, they discussed it for a time. Dorothy seemed to have so much joy as heaven was described and discussed.

He could see it on her face.

That was not the last time they talked about heaven, that wonderful place in the presence of God where Jesus has prepared a place for all those who have cast their cares on Him and put their trust in Him.

Dorothy's condition began to worsen, and Pastor Bombay learned that she had a very advanced case of terminal cancer. She suffered with a great deal of pain and remembered the words from Revelation 21:4, "There shall be no more pain...." She knew she was dying and was quite ready to talk about it. She was quite prepared for the end here, and the beginning there.

She told Pastor Bombay, "Before you told me about heaven, I was afraid, since I didn't know what would happen to me when I died. No one ever told me or read to me about heaven and what to expect. Now I am not afraid anymore. I have a lot of pain, and I would like to go to that beautiful place *there*."

The next visit Dick scheduled never came about, since she had gone on to be *there* with the Lord.

Dorothy had died, but she had the peace and joy of knowing her final destination. Why do we wait until funerals to speak about this place called heaven? The only reliable source of knowledge we have about heaven is the Bible. True, it may bring comfort to mourners at the funeral of a Christian friend, but how much more comfort and peace it gives to the believer before death and the funeral!

Dorothy had the peace that comes through faith, and not through sight!

27

Retirement

Dick tried to retire several times, but it never seemed to take root. Even when he moved back to Oshawa where he had pastored for so long, he was most often out in ministry – filling in for a few weeks while a pastor was on holiday or when a church was searching for a new pastor. He would go out by invitation and do biblical seminars starting on a Friday evening, through Saturday and Sunday. The subject often was "Divine Healing According to the Word."

He would teach, but not pray for the sick. On the final session or meeting on a Sunday, he would then simply point out the Scripture in James 5:14, where it says, "Is anyone among you sick? Let him call for the elders of the church, and let them pray over him, anointing him with oil in the name of the Lord." Then he'd stand back, and let the Church do what the Church should do on a regular basis. Phenomenal healings would take place as the local elders simply obeyed God as they prayed for those who called on them to pray. No fanfare, just simple faith.

In 1980, with retirement firmly in mind, Dick and Olive went to Britain for a month, visiting friends they had met over the years. And, of course, doing a little bit of preaching. They were guests of the Assemblies of God Conference held at the Butlins Camp near Minehead, Devon, on the Bristol Channel.

All the towns in the area were ancient and filled with history, so they did the tourist thing, seeing as much as possible. They saw an old church high up on a hill, and while browsing about, they met two white-haired ladies. One of them casually remarked that it was much warmer here than where they lived in Bolton, north-west of Manchester.

Dick told them that they intended to visit an old friend in Bolton. They asked his name. Bolton is a big city, and the chances of them knowing someone Dick and Olive knew would be astronomical. Dick gave them his name, Bill Vell. The ladies asked if he was a minister and Dick affirmed that he was. They said, "We know him."

He had held a meeting in their church, and after preaching, he had prayed for those who needed healing. One of the two ladies had gone forward for prayer and was healed. They thought him to be a wonderful young man.

Then Dick told them this story, just as it had happened:

"Bill Vell lived with his widowed mother in Nairobi, Kenya. His mother and her sister attended the Nairobi Evangelistic Centre where I pastored. The sister's husband was very ill and they asked for prayer for him in the service. They also asked if I could visit the sick man in the hospital after the meeting.

"As soon as I could leave I went to the hospital. The two sisters and Bill Vell met me at the entrance. They told me that the man had already died. I gave the widow what comfort I could and prayed with them in the darkness outside the hospital. Young Bill Vell was standing by.

"Bill began attending services where I pastored, was saved and filled with the Holy Ghost. He immediately began serving God in any and every way he could. He became the leader of our young people's group and sometimes led the song service during the Sunday meetings.

"Shortly, he told me that he felt he wanted to be a minister, asking what training was required. I suggested the Assemblies of God College in England, since there was no adequate training for ministers in Kenya at the time. He went, graduated, and became a minister in Britain, pastoring in Bolton."

One day, Bill Vell told Dick how it all came about. Bill had not known Dick until the night his uncle had died. When Dick had stood praying in the dark with his mother and his aunt, God spoke to him that he was to become a minister "like that man" who prayed with such compassion. Bill heard and obeyed. God used him greatly.

Of such chance meetings moments of joy are made.

28

The End

One Sunday, Mary, my wife, and I felt that we should skip church that day and go to spend time with my father and mother, Dick and Olive. It was May 8, Mother's Day, 1994. Dad had been having a few problems with heart palpitations and had been in the hospital, but he was stabilized and had come home the previous Friday.

To our surprise, when we got to their apartment in Oshawa, my brother Rick and his wife, Wendy, as well as my sister Ruth and her daughter, Barbara, had already arrived, with the same thoughts. Mother's Day and a chance to visit with convalescent Dad again. Then, my own son, John, with his wife, Karen, and their active little boy, Josh, turned up only moments later. We were all a surprise to each other.

Visits with Dad always seemed to revolve around the things of

God, the ministry, and, of course, family. This time was no different.

It seemed like a full house, but Dad, who was now eighty-four and often disturbed by too much activity and particularly noise, sat quietly smiling in his favourite chair. We talked about everything. As lunch time came and went, we each seemed to take turns gravitating toward the chair next to Dad. He seemed tired, but not feeble, and was obviously enjoying our company.

We all left late in the afternoon.

The following Thursday, Mom called to say Dad was back in the hospital. He had complained of chest pains. Mom had wanted to call an ambulance, but Dad declined. He didn't want to be a burden to anyone, his usual attitude. Dad dressed and walked to the car. Mom drove to the hospital, where he walked in the front door. The nurses were slightly scolding, saying he should have come in an ambulance, or at least waited for a wheelchair.

Dad began to sink slowly but surely, and by the time I arrived, he had slipped into unconsciousness. But before he slipped into the coma, he was experiencing a great deal of discomfort as he lay unable to move. With his last words, he neither made a deep spiritual statement nor did he relay any requests or instructions – that had already been done. Dad was ready for death.

Instead, he hailed back to one of his most often made criticisms when some song leader would ask everyone to stand and change their positions. (How could you stand without changing your position?) In his discomfort, and ready to stand in the presence of God, he said, "I wish I could stand to change my position!" His last words.

All the sons and daughters had arrived except Ruth, who was still on her way from Detroit.

A heart monitor was set up in the room. It began to show less and less strength. One of us asked that it be shut off, since it seemed a morbid, mechanical intrusion on a family about to face the death of the dearest man in their lives.

With a last slow breath, Dad's spirit left his body. Mother fell across Dad's lifeless body with one heart-wrenching call, "Oh, Dick!" We all wept at the loss of a man who had been the world to all of us. He was now standing, his position changed from a death bed to standing in the presence of the One he had served faithfully all his life.

We lead Mom out and went back to her apartment. "Her" apartment now.

Dad had left a few requests about his funeral. They were all honoured.

It was a rare kind of funeral. The church was absolutely packed. Dignitaries from the city of Oshawa and the P.A.O.C. attended to honour a man who had honoured God from the day he was born again.

There were tough moments. My brothers, David and Rick, and I were to sing a trio, with our cousin Ken Bombay playing the piano. While trying to practice "All the Way My Saviour Leads Me," we never made it through the song once. Emotions would not allow. We sat and remembered. Yet during the service, there was a sense of triumph, and we sang it through without any problem other than the fear that we *would* have a problem. There was, as Dad would have wanted, a sense of victory, triumph, and even moments of great humour during the service.

The interment ended with one of the strangest, but most fitting gestures by my sister Lois. It was a cool day, and she had grabbed one of Dad's spring overcoats to wear at the graveside. When she put her hand in one of the pockets, she felt two objects. A toothpick and a washer. Just after the pastor had said his final words and prayed, Lois looked at me with a glint in her eye, glanced at the rest of the family, then reached over and placed them on top of the casket.

It may have seemed both strange and out of place to most who were there, but to us, the family, it had a very deep and humourous meaning. The washer seemed like a symbol of Dick Bombay, the practical man, who dirtied his hands to build, work, garden, and fix his kids' toys. The toothpick reminded us all of the humourous habit Dad had. He'd break off a quarter-inch of a toothpick, grip it by the ends between his teeth, then with the rest of the toothpick, flick it across the room at one of us. It was almost like a kiss.

Thus ended the life of a man, a very physical man and a deeply spiritual man; loved by everyone who ever knew him. From a rocky dirt farm and bare feet, through a life of service to all men, he now stood clothed in his final robe of righteousness in the presence of God.

It was many months after Dick's death that Olive was emotionally able to start looking through his papers. He often scribbled thoughts and ideas on little pieces of paper. One Olive found and kept in a drawer of his desk. In Dick's handwriting was scrawled, "I shall be satisfied when I awake in His likeness. John, still in the body, fell down as dead when he saw the glorified Jesus. When we are raised at His coming, we will be completely satisfied – perhaps for the first time in all our previous existence. What perfect peace, fulfilled joy... everything set right!"

A Man Worth Knowing!

By the Same Author

The Right Stuff, Volume 1

The Right Stuff, Volume 2

The Right Stuff, Volume 3

The Wisdom of Nature

Practical Thoughts on Romans

A View From the Barn

Let My People Go!

God, Down to Earth

COMING SOON!

A novel set in 1820, for eight to twelve-year-old children,
involving a black slave, a native Canadian Indian,
and a white Methodist preacher's son. The first of a series.

For more information, contact:
Cal R. Bombay
R.R. #1
Brantford, Ontario, Canada
N3T 5L4